Cookies *for* Christmas

D0387040

Also by Maria Robbins

The Dumpling Cookbook
American Corn
Blue-Ribbon Cookies
Blue-Ribbon Pies
Blue-Ribbon Pickles and Preserves
A Cook's Alphabet of Quotations
The Christmas Companion (with Jim Charlton)
A Gardener's Bouquet of Quotations

Cookies *for* Christmas

Maria Robbins

• • •

Illustrations by Durell Godfrey

ST. MARTIN'S PRESS ♦ NEW YORK

Library of Congress Cataloging-in-Publication Data

Polushkin, Maria.
   Cookies for Christmas / Maria Robbins.
     p.   cm.
   ISBN 0-312-09775-1 (pbk.)
   1. Cookies. 2. Christmas cookery. I. Title.
TX772.P69 1993
641.8′654—dc20   93-21622
                                   CIP

10 9 8 7 6 5 4 3

This book is dedicated to my Aunt Tamara, who sends me her wonderful homemade cookies for Christmas, just as she has through all the years of her life.

◆ ◆ ◆

I want very much to thank Robyn Low for sharing recipes, kitchen time, advice, and wonderful meals. Other friends were equally generous with recipes and moral support: thank you Winnie Rosen, Genie Chipps, Bobs Strachan, Ann Mann, Hildy Maze, and Gary Rieveschl. Special thanks to Durell Godfrey for her drawings, and to Tim Lee for his wonderful photography. My editor, Barbara Anderson, continues to be invaluable for her careful readings and excellent advice. And finally, as always and ever, I am grateful to Faith Hamlin for representation, Lydia for sorority, and my husband Ken for everything else.

Contents

Cookies for Christmas — 1
How to Bake the Perfect Christmas Cookie — 13
One-Step Cookies — 23

These cookies are started and completed in one session. You mix the dough, shape the cookies, and bake them.

Christmas Shortbread — 25
Fancy Spritz Cookies — 28
Ann Mann's Mexican Christmas Cookies — 30
Rolled Almond Christmas Wafers — 32
Oatmeal Lace Cookies — 34
Maple Walnut Cookies — 36
Ginger Snaps — 38
Robyn's Chocolate "Oh"s — 40
Grown-Up Chocolate Chip Cookies — 42
The Best Fudgy Brownies — 44
Chocolate Madeleines — 46
Choco-Coco Kisses — 48
Chocolate Hazelnut Macaroons — 50
Coffee Meringue Kisses — 52

Raspberry Linzer Hearts 54
Jam-Filled Thimble Cookies 56
Orange-Almond Tuiles 58
Christmas Oatmeal Cookies 60
Oatmeal, Raisin, Cranberry, Pecan, Chocolate Chip Cookies 62
Walnut Kisses 64
Caraway Seed Cookies 66
Vanilla Wafers 68
Cinnamon Mandelbröt 70

Two-Step Cookies 73

*These cookies are prepared in two sessions. The dough is mixed
and refrigerated, or shaped and allowed to stand overnight to dry.
The baking takes place after 2 to 12 hours.*

Old-Fashioned Sugar Cookies 75
Springerle Cookies 80
A Gingerbread Menagerie 83
Jan Hagel Cookies 88
Pfeffernüsse 90
Fancy Lemon Butter Cookies 92
Rosemary Shortbread Cookies 96
Almond Crescents 98
Chocolate Brownie Cookies 100
Savory Cheese Cookies 102
Chocolate Teddy Bears 104

Confections and Other Goodies 107

    Chocolate Truffles 109
    Genie's Kentucky Bourbon Balls 111
    Candied Citrus Peel 112
    Candied Cranberries 115
    Candied Ginger 117
    Walnut Brittle 119
    Vanilla Brandy 121
    Vanilla Sugar 122
    Vanilla Confectioners' Sugar 123

Mail Order Sources for Equipment and Supplies 125
Index 129

Cookies for
Christmas

I hate Christmas. I hate all the hullaballoo. I hate shopping. I hate most of the tinny-sounding music. I hate spending a lot of money on presents that nobody needs or wants. I hate the idea of cutting down trees and bringing them indoors. I hate the Caribbean. I hate to ski. I am a Christmas curmudgeon, prone to getting the Christmastime blues. But I have found my salvation, the solution to almost every problem during this midwinter madness— I bake cookies. Starting in early December and continuing right through the holidays, I bake hundreds and hundreds, dozens and dozens of small, delicious, variously shaped and colored cookies. My shopping spree is limited to the grocery store, where I buy sacks of flour and sugar, pounds of butter, and dozens of eggs. Mail order sources provide me with excellent chocolate, an assortment of sprinkles and glitters, and with raisins, dried cherries, cranberries, figs, and so on. I stock up on tins and cardboard boxes, as well as my own choice of music tapes and audiocassettes of long novels read aloud by wonderful actors. My kitchen becomes my haven and my workshop, and for several days and nights every week I bake cookies. I wrap them up as packages to replace greeting cards and all other Christmas gifts. It's hard to be depressed surrounded by wonderful tastes and aromas, and a box of homebaked cookies hardly ever fails to please the recipient of the gift. You might find it funny that when someone gives *me* a gift of Christmas cookies I'm just as pleased as punch, but by that time it's great to eat a cookie made by someone else.

Over the years I've kept a recipe collection of my favorite cookies for Christmas—cookies relatively easy to bake, sturdy enough to hang as ornaments or to survive a cross-country postal journey, and cookies that look stunning with very little effort or expense.

In this book you'll find thirty-four of my all-time favorites, as well as eight recipes for the special condiments and sweets that can add sparkle to any holiday table or gift. I hope you'll try them all, and enjoy them for both yourself and your family, and as gifts for special friends.

On the following pages you'll find ways to help you get organized for holiday baking, and ideas on how to package your cookies for Christmas gift giving.

GETTING ORGANIZED FOR HOLIDAY COOKIE BAKING

Soon after Thanksgiving, sit down and make some lists. Make a list of everyone to whom you'd like to give cookies for Christmas. From that list, make a separate list of people who don't live nearby and to whom you will need to send cookies. Look through the following lists and the recipes in this book to match up cookies with people. Make a final list of which cookies need to be baked first so that you have plenty of time to send them.

COOKIES AND CONFECTIONS THAT CAN BE MADE AT LEAST THREE WEEKS IN ADVANCE

These are cookies and confections whose flavor actually improves with time. Bake these first, then store them in airtight containers to be well prepared for the season ahead.

Ginger Snaps (page 38)
Cinnamon Mandelbröt (page 70)

Springerle Cookies (page 80)
A Gingerbread Menagerie (page 83)
Jan Hagel Cookies (page 88)
Pfeffernüsse (page 90)
Candied Citrus Peel (page 112)
Candied Cranberries (page 115)
Candied Ginger (page 117)
Walnut Brittle (page 119)
Vanilla Brandy (page 121)
Vanilla Sugar (page 122)
Vanilla Confectioners' Sugar (page 123)

COOKIES AND CONFECTIONS THAT SHIP WELL

Save yourself and the recipient a disappointment and avoid shipping cookies that are fragile or have a very short keeping time. The following cookies are all sturdy enough to travel if they are carefully packed.

Fancy Spritz Cookies (page 28)
Ann Mann's Mexican Christmas Cookies (page 30)
Maple Walnut Cookies (page 36)
Ginger Snaps (page 38)
Grown-Up Chocolate Chip Cookies (page 42)
The Best Fudgy Brownies (page 44)
Chocolate Madeleines (page 46)
Choco-Coco Kisses (page 48)

Chocolate Hazelnut Macaroons (page 50)
Christmas Oatmeal Cookies (page 60)
Oatmeal, Raisin, Cranberry, Pecan, Chocolate Chip Cookies (page 62)
Walnut Kisses (page 64)
Caraway Seed Cookies (page 66)
Vanilla Wafers (page 68)
Cinnamon Mandelbröt (page 70)
Old-Fashioned Sugar Cookies (page 75)
Springerle Cookies (page 80)
A Gingerbread Menagerie (page 83)
Jan Hagel Cookies (page 88)
Pfeffernüsse (page 90)
Fancy Lemon Butter Cookies (page 92)
Almond Crescents (page 98)
Chocolate Brownie Cookies (page 100)
Savory Cheese Cookies (page 102)
Chocolate Teddy Bears (page 104)
Genie's Kentucky Bourbon Balls (page 111)
Candied Citrus Peel (page 112)
Candied Cranberries (page 115)
Candied Ginger (page 117)
Walnut Brittle (page 119)

A COOKIE-BAKING TIMETABLE

RIGHT AFTER THANKSGIVING

- make lists
- gather recipes
- place mail orders for spices, flavorings, decorative sugars, dragées, edible glitter and gold, and food coloring
- clean out freezer and refrigerator
- check stock of plastic containers, tins, or special gift containers
- check cookie sheets (I buy one or two new ones each year)
- buy flour, sugar, butter, chocolate, nuts, parchment paper, and so on
- purchase tissue paper, wax paper, tin foil
- gather cookie cutters
- collect ribbons to hang cookie ornaments
- locate pastry bag, decorative tips, and paint brushes for decorating

FIRST WEEK OF DECEMBER

- start baking cookies
- gather wrapping material and shipping cartons
- gather packing material
- gather labels and package sealing tape

SECOND WEEK OF DECEMBER

- continue baking cookies
- start mailing packages for Christmas delivery

THIRD WEEK OF DECEMBER

- bake cookies like crazy
- bake cookies for tree decorations
- buy and decorate tree
- send packages you didn't send last week

LAST DAYS BEFORE CHRISTMAS

- bake cookies for hand-delivered presents
- package and wrap cookies you baked three weeks ago
- send packages by expensive delivery services because you didn't do it last week

CHRISTMAS

- relax and have a cookie

HOW TO PACK AND SHIP COOKIES SO THEY ARRIVE IN GOOD CONDITION

1. **Select the right cookie container**. Cookie tins, sturdy boxes with lids such as hat boxes, and plastic containers with tight-fitting lids are all excellent containers for shipping cookies. Keep in mind that the container becomes part of the gift, so match the container to the person. A special friend might love a flowered hat box while a more practical one would be very happy with a large, reusable plastic container. (Somehow, no kitchen ever has enough of these.) In a pinch a sturdy cardboard box, such as those sold at post offices, will do very well.

2. **Stock up on tissue paper and wax paper**. These two items are your friends. Tissue paper provides insulation as well as a festive look. Insulate your cookie container with several layers of tissue paper on the bottom and top, then layer wax paper between each layer of cookies. Close the container and use tape to secure the lid. Additional gift wrapping is up to you.

3. **Assemble your mailing cartons and packing material**. Mailing cartons should be made of heavy cardboard and be substantially larger than your cookie container so that there is room for packing material to insulate the cookies from the harsh outside world. There are a lot of excellent packing materials around: Crumpled-up newspaper is cheap and easy to come by; crumpled-up tissue paper is fine; popped (unbuttered) popcorn is excellent and biodegradable; styrofoam peanuts and bubble wrap are very effective, although ecologically unsound. Whatever you use, there should be several inches of packing material between all sides of the mailing carton and the cookie container inside.

PACKAGING IDEAS FOR COOKIES DELIVERED BY HAND

Cookies that you will be delivering by hand, either as Christmas gifts, contributions to an evening's entertainment, or as gifts for your dinner host or hostess can be packaged in a great variety of ways. Here are some ideas:

- decorative cookie tins
- antique cookie jars
- large glass wide-mouthed jars with cork stoppers and glass decanters
- decorative plates and platters wrapped with colored cellophane and curled ribbon
- Chinese food take-out containers lined with colored tissue paper
- pretty hat boxes lined with tissue paper
- woven baskets lined with tissue paper and wrapped with colored cellophane

For special gifts, add one of the following to a batch of cookies:

- a set of special cookie cutters tied together with a ribbon
- a shortbread mold
- an antique cookie stamp
- a springerle mold
- a small attractive book of Christmas cookie recipes

COOKIES AS ORNAMENTS

The following cookie recipes make excellent, long-lasting ornaments for Christmas trees and, as a bonus, remain edible.

- Old-Fashioned Sugar Cookies (page 75)
- Springerle Cookies (page 80)
- A Gingerbread Menagerie (page 83)
- Chocolate Teddy Bears (page 104)

Most of the cookies on nineteenth-century Christmas trees were thicker than today's cookies: Spice, butter, and gingerbread cookies were often half an inch thick. White cookies were frequently sprinkled with red sugar, "for pretty," as the Pennsylvania Dutch still say. Cookie baking binges often lasted for two solid weeks early in December. A "washbasketful" was a standard of measure for cookies in Pennsylvania Dutch kitchens. The housewife who didn't have at least several washbaskets full of cookies just wasn't ready for Christmas.

—*The Christmas Tree Book*, by Phillip V. Snyder

CHRISTMAS COOKIE TRADITION

Cookies of one sort or another have been a part of religious rites and celebrations in nearly every country of the world for thousands of years. Long before there was a Christmas, there were winter festivals. In the darkest, most barren time of the year, they included the lighting of bonfires, oil lamps, and candles to help the sun survive the darkness, and the sacrifice of animals to ensure the return of spring. Centuries later, instead of live animals, people offered their gods small cakes of grain in the shapes of the animals—the original animal crackers, you might say. Consider the still-popular German Christmas cookie called the springerle. Its name means *little jumper* and it recalls the Julfest, an ancient holiday during which a living horse was sacrificed to Wotan, the chief German god.

Of course, winter festivals were not limited to sacrifices. For thousands of years people have given small gifts to friends and neighbors, often including honey cakes to make the coming year sweeter. The tradition of a decorated tree only added to the merriment and provided a place to hang small treats, including cookies.

How to Bake the Perfect Christmas Cookie

One of the wonderful things about cookies is that they provide enjoyment far in excess of the effort it takes to make them. If you follow just a few of the simple guidelines outlined below, you'll find these recipes to be virtually failproof, yielding great-tasting and attractive cookies with a minimum of time and fuss.

1. Read the recipe.
2. Assemble equipment and ingredients.
3. Preheat oven and check oven temperature.
4. Prepare cookie sheets as directed in recipe.
5. Measure carefully.
6. Mix the dough according to directions.
7. Don't skip refrigerating the dough if this is called for in the instructions.
8. Halfway through baking time, rearrange the cookie sheets, rotating them top to bottom and back to front, to ensure even baking.
9. Remove cookies from cookie sheets as soon as they are firm enough to move. Cool them completely on wire cooling racks.
10. Be sure to cool cookie sheets completely between baking batches of cookies. You can do this quickly by running cold water over them, or placing them outside the kitchen door for a few minutes.

EQUIPMENT

Electric mixer. Most of the recipes in this book call for an electric mixer. A heavy-duty stationary-stand mixer is a wonderful tool in the kitchen, but a portable hand mixer is perfectly fine.

Food processor. Some recipes call for the use of a food processor. It is used to pulverize sugar, nuts, chocolate, etc., and to cut butter into dry ingredients.

Saucepan and double boiler. A heavyweight saucepan is needed to reduce syrups, and a double boiler is necessary for melting chocolate. If these are coated with a nonstick surface, all the better for you when it comes time to clean up.

Measuring cups. You should have two kinds—a set of metal or plastic nesting cups with flat rims for dry ingredients, and glass measuring cups with a pouring spout and clear markings for liquid ingredients.

Measuring spoons. It is useful to have at least two sets of standard, graduated measuring spoons.

Mixing bowls. Have an assortment of large, medium, and small mixing bowls.

Wire whisk. Whisks are useful for blending flour with other dry ingredients, but if you don't have one you can use a fork.

Wooden spoons and rubber spatulas. Wooden spoons are used for hand mixing, rubber spatulas for folding solid ingredients into a batter.

Rolling pin and pastry cloth. A sturdy rolling pin is essential and a pastry cloth is a great help. Invest in a heavy, hardwood rolling pin with ball bearings. A pastry cloth is inexpensive and can be ordered from baking catalogs such as *Maid of Scandinavia* or *The King Arthur Flour Baker's Catalogue* (see page 127 for address information).

Cookie cutters. You will want to have an assortment of cookie cutters on hand. I collect cookie cutters all year round, searching them out at flea markets, yard sales, and specialty cooking stores like *The Bridge Company* and *Williams-Sonoma* (see page 127 for address information).

Cookie press with an assortment of disks. Only one recipe (Fancy Spritz Cookies, page 28) calls for the use of a cookie press. If you don't have a cookie press, you can use a pastry bag or settle for cookies that are delicious but look rather ordinary.

Pastry bag with a few large and small tips. A pastry bag is an inexpensive and useful item in the kitchen. Many people are resistant to using one, considering it too much trouble or too fussy. It really is neither. It takes no great skill to use and yields extremely professional-looking results. A simple substitute for a pastry bag is a large freezer bag (quart or gallon size). Snip off a small piece from a corner of the bag and insert a decorating tube.

Cookie sheets. Use heavy-weight, shiny, metal cookie sheets. Avoid dark-colored baking sheets. Edges should be flat or barely turned up, so that heat can reach cookies evenly from all directions. Insulated baking sheets are fine, but they will require a slightly longer baking time—usually the maximum baking time given in the recipe. Nonstick baking sheets are fine if made of heavy-weight metal and coated with a top-quality nonstick material. (If any of your baking sheets are light and flimsy, do yourself a favor and throw them out.) If you are short of cookie sheets and want to use a jelly roll pan, turn it upside down and use that side; otherwise, the raised edges will impede the flow of air to the cookies.

Baking parchment. This is an indispensable aid in my kitchen. It eliminates the need to grease cookie sheets or to ever clean them again. I dislike the parchment that comes in rolls and buy it in sheets from *Maid of Scandinavia* (see page 127 for address information). I find that I can use a sheet of parchment two or three times before discarding it. Aluminum foil (shiny-side up) can be used instead of baking parchment in many recipes.

Oven thermometer. I've never found an oven that wasn't several degrees off, and an oven thermometer makes it possible for you to adjust the difference. Put the thermometer in the center of the oven when you turn it on. Wait 15 minutes to check the temperature and make the necessary adjustment. If the discrepancy is more than 50°F, you should have your oven recalibrated by an authorized service agent.

Timer. The only time I ever burned an entire batch of cookies was when I tried to bake without a timer. Set your timer to go off in the minimum baking time, so you can check the cookies and decide whether to leave them in or take them out.

Wire cooling racks. Raised wire racks allow cookies to cool quickly because the air reaches them from all directions. If you are baking large quantities of cookies at a time, make your life easier by having enough cooling racks for all your cookies. Cookies must be cooled completely before they can be stored.

Spatulas. You will find it useful to have several kinds of spatulas. A narrow metal spatula is used for leveling off dry ingredients; for transferring unbaked, cutout cookies to a baking sheet; and for loosening the edges of cookies like brownies or shortbread from a pan. A wide flexible metal spatula is used to remove baked cookies from the baking sheets to a cooling rack. Rubber spatulas are used to scrape down the sides of a mixing bowl.

Strainers. Use a large metal strainer to remove any lumps from confectioners' sugar and brown sugar. Use a small fine-meshed strainer for sifting confectioners' sugar over baked cookies and for straining the pulp from lemon juice.

Brushes. Have a selection of artist's brushes on hand for painting and decorating cookies.

Plastic wrap. This is essential for wrapping up cookie dough that needs refrigeration before rolling out.

Wax paper. Wax paper is excellent for laying between cookies when they are stored.

Cookie storage containers. These fall into two categories: (1) very useful and ugly, and (2) pretty but useless for long-term storage. For storage at home I use the former—plastic containers with very airtight lids. For gift wrapping and sending, I collect cookie tins. These are usually attractive, but I have never found one with a really airtight lid. My assumption, however, is that the recipient will consume the cookies long before the inadequacy of the lid has any effect on the cookies.

INGREDIENTS

Flour. All-purpose flour is called for in a great majority of the recipes. You can use either bleached or unbleached flour, as I have not found a noticeable difference in the way they perform in these recipes. Measure flour by spooning it lightly into a measuring cup until it overflows, then level the top with the edge of a metal spatula or knife. Do not tap the measuring cup to make the flour settle or try to press it in; this will make your measurement inaccurate.

Butter. With only one or two exceptions, I use butter in all the recipes in this book, and I use only sweet (unsalted) high-fat-content butter. (Land O Lakes is the best brand available in supermarkets across the country.) When preparing to bake cookies, buy butter in quantity and store it in the freezer.

Sugar. Granulated sugar is measured exactly like flour. Brown or light brown sugar is measured by pressing sugar down firmly until the cup is filled to the rim, then leveling with the edge of a metal spatula or knife. Confectioners' sugar should be strained through a coarse sieve to remove lumps, spooned lightly into a measuring cup, then leveled with the edge of a metal spatula or knife.

Eggs. Large eggs are called for in all recipes. Remove them from the refrigerator 30 minutes before using.

Nuts. Use unsalted nuts. Store all nuts in the refrigerator or freezer to prevent them from going rancid. Toasting nuts brings out their flavor and is called for in several recipes. To toast nuts, preheat oven to 350°F. Spread the nuts in a single layer in a shallow baking pan. Bake until nuts are very hot and have a definite aroma—usually between 10 and 15 minutes. Cool completely and remove any loose skin before using or storing.

Nuts can be ground or very finely chopped in a food processor. I find it helps to add a tablespoon of sugar to the processor to keep the nuts from becoming sticky. To coarsely chop nuts, use a sharp long-bladed chef's knife.

Chocolate. Be sure to use the type of chocolate called for in the recipe— unsweetened, bittersweet, or semisweet—and use the best quality you can find.

Cocoa. Use the type of cocoa called for, usually an unsweetened cocoa powder.

Vanilla extract and other flavorings. In recipes calling for vanilla or almond extract or any other extract flavoring, please use the ones labeled *pure extract* and avoid any with the word *imitation* on the label.

Oatmeal. Always use plain rolled oats (sometimes called old-fashioned oats), not the quick-cooking or instant type.

Nonstick vegetable cooking spray. If you do not use parchment paper or tin foil to line your cookie sheets, I recommend using a nonstick vegetable cooking spray to grease your cookie sheets.

STORING YOUR COOKIES

- Plastic storage containers with tight-fitting lids are best.
- Cookie tins are less airtight but more attractive. These are better for gift giving.
- Store each type of cookie by itself. Don't mix soft and crisp cookies together—the crisp ones will quickly become soft.
- If soft cookies are drying out, you can add moisture by placing half an apple in the container with the cookies. Let stand for a day or two, then remove the apple.
- If cookies are going soft from standing around, place them on a cookie sheet and bake in a preheated 350°F oven for 3 to 4 minutes to crisp them. Transfer the cookies to a wire rack to cool. Let them cool completely before storing.
- Keep cookies from breaking by placing sheets of wax paper on the bottom and top of the container and between each layer.

WHAT ABOUT FREEZING?

- Most cookies can be frozen for up to three months. After that time the flavor starts to deteriorate. Freeze cookies in small batches in plastic self-sealing freezer bags. To defrost, remove cookies from the bag and arrange on a plate. Cookies will thaw at room temperature in about 20 minutes.

- I prefer to freeze the unbaked cookie dough because it takes up much less space than the finished cookies. Remove cookie dough from the freezer, let it thaw to the temperature required in the recipe, then proceed.

General advice for entertaining carolers: Keep everything as small as possible, so that it is easy to eat without crumbs everywhere. Don't try to be original. In my experience, clever food is not appreciated at Christmas. It makes the little ones cry and the old ones nervous.

—Jane Grigson

One-Step Cookies

These cookies are started and completed in one session. You mix the dough, shape the cookies, and bake them.

⋅ CHRISTMAS SHORTBREAD ⋅

Shortbread comes from Scotland where it is eaten all year round, but particularly at Christmastime and for Hogmanay, the Scottish New Year celebration. Originally, shortbread was a large round cake, with spokes notched like rays radiating out from the center to symbolize the rays of the sun. Today, shortbread comes in many varieties. It can be baked in special molds that will imprint designs in the cake, and cut into pieces after it is baked. Lacking a mold, it can be baked in a round cake pan, scored, and cut into triangles after baking. Incidentally, in the eighteenth century these triangles were called "Petticoat Tails," for they were thought to resemble the scalloped shape of a lady's petticoats.

Shortbread can be decorated with colored sugars, candied lemon zest, caraway seeds, and finely chopped almonds. But I prefer it left to its lovely, pure, buttery color, although occasionally I will sprinkle the top with granulated sugar before baking, just to give it a nice sheen.

2 cups all-purpose flour
½ cup vanilla confectioners' sugar
  (page 123)
2 sticks sweet butter, refrigerator
  cold

Optional:
2 tablespoons granulated sugar for
  topping

Equipment: *food processor or electric mixer; 2 8-inch round cake pans or shortbread pans*; wire cooling racks*

1. Preheat oven to 275 to 300°F.

2. Sift flour and sugar together and put into a food processor with a metal blade. With food processor on, add butter in small pieces and process just until mixture turns to crumbly bits.

3. Scrape out of food-processor bowl into a plastic bag. Mash together into a ball. Remove ball from bag and place on a lightly floured surface and knead until mixture just holds together. Handle the dough as little as possible.

4. Divide the dough into 2 equal parts. Lightly press each piece of dough into an 8-inch-round cake pan or shortbread pan. Crimp the edges of the dough with the tines of a fork so they resemble the rays of the sun. Use the fork to prick the dough all over so it does not blister. Mark the circle with a knife to indicate 8 wedges, but do not cut through the dough. Sprinkle a tablespoon of sugar over each circle of dough. If you own decorative short-bread pans, use them, and follow their directions. If you are baking only one pan at a time, keep the remaining dough wrapped and refrigerated.

5. It will take approximately 1 hour to bake the shortbread. Bake for 30 minutes without disturbing. Check to see that the shortbread is baking evenly.

---

*You can purchase beautiful shortbread pans through these catalogs:

The King Arthur Flour Baker's Catalogue
RR 2, Box 56
Norwich, Vermont 05055
(800) 827–6836

Maid of Scandinavia
3244 Raleigh Avenue
Minneapolis, Minnesota 55416
(800) 328–6722

Move pans around in the oven. Bake 30 minutes more, checking on them in about 20 minutes. Shortbread should be pale with a light golden tint around the edges.

6. Remove from oven. Let cool in pans on wire rack for 10 to 15 minutes. Remove shortbread from pans while still slightly warm by inverting the pan onto a wooden cutting board and tapping smartly on the bottom of the pan. Cut shortbread into 8 wedges. Alternately, cut shortbread into wedges while still in pans, loosen sides with a knife, and lift wedges out one at a time. Cool wedges on wire racks. Store completely cooled shortbread in airtight container.

Yield: 16 wedges of shortbread
Will keep: 1 month at room temperature

Using an electric mixer: Remove butter from refrigerator 30 minutes before using to soften. In a large bowl, cream butter with an electric mixer at medium speed. Increase speed and gradually beat in sugar. Continue beating until mixture is light and fluffy. On low speed, beat in flour mixture until just incorporated.

Christmas won't be Christmas without any presents.
—Louisa May Alcott

· FANCY SPRITZ COOKIES ·

Everybody's aunt or grandmother used to make these for the holidays, and no wonder. They are pretty, festive, and keep extremely well. They are good for sending, and to have around the house arranged on a Christmas plate. I like them because I finally get to use the cookie press that lives untouched in my baking cupboard the rest of the year. The recipe for these cookies comes from my friend Hildy's grandmother, Adeline Amdury.

2 cups all-purpose flour
¼ teaspoon salt
½ cup sugar
½ cup blanched almonds, roughly chopped
2 sticks sweet butter
1 large egg
1 teaspoon vanilla extract
1 teaspoon almond extract

Toppings:
Candied Cranberries (page 115), whole blanched almonds, glacé cherries, colored sugars, or dragées

Equipment: food processor or electric mixer; cookie press; cookie sheets, lined with parchment paper or lightly greased; wire cooling racks

1. Preheat oven to 375°F.

2. In a small bowl, stir flour and salt with a wire whisk, to blend. Set aside.

3. In a food processor with a metal blade, process the sugar and almonds for several minutes until their texture becomes very fine. With the processor on, add the butter in small pieces and process until smooth and creamy.

Scrape down sides of bowl, add the egg, vanilla extract, and almond extract and process until completely incorporated. Scrape down sides of bowl again, add flour mixture, and process until just blended.

4. Pack dough into cookie press. Keep unused portion of dough in refrigerator. Press out desired shapes on prepared cookie sheet. Space the cookies 1 inch apart. Decorate centers with Candied Cranberries, whole blanched almonds, glacé cherries, colored sugars, or dragées.

5. Bake 10 to 12 minutes, until cookies are pale gold in color. Remove from oven and transfer cookies to wire racks to cool. Store completely cooled cookies in an airtight container.

Yield: about 4 dozen cookies
Will keep: 1 month at room temperature

Using an electric mixer: Take butter out of refrigerator 30 minutes before using to soften. In a nut grinder or food processor grind the almonds to a powder-fine consistency. In a large bowl, cream the butter with an electric mixer at medium speed. Raise speed to high and gradually beat in the sugar. Continue beating until mixture is light and fluffy. Beat in egg, vanilla extract, and almond extract until completely incorporated. Reduce beater speed to low; gradually beat in the flour and ground almonds.

· ANN MANN'S MEXICAN CHRISTMAS COOKIES ·

Last year, just before Christmas, I was spending a few days with my sister when her neighbor, Ann Mann, stopped in to deliver a beautiful tin of Christmas cookies. One bite and I was in love. I've tasted many similar cookies but never ones so melt-in-the-mouth delicious as these. Ann, it turns out, grew up in Mazatlan, Mexico, where her mother baked these cookies by the thousands and sold them to put her children through school.

2 sticks sweet butter, softened
2 sticks margarine, softened
½ cup sugar
3 teaspoons vanilla
4 cups all-purpose flour, sifted
   twice

2 cups finely chopped pecans
Vanilla confectioners' sugar (page
   123) or plain confectioners' sugar

Equipment: electric mixer; ungreased
cookie sheets

1. Preheat oven to 350°F.

2. In a large bowl, with an electric mixer at medium speed, cream together butter, margarine, sugar, and vanilla until very light and fluffy.

3. Measure out 2⅔ cups of flour and dump it all at once into the creamed mixture. Blend with electric mixer, at low speed, for 5 seconds until barely blended.

4. Sprinkle the nuts over the dough and sprinkle the additional flour over the dough. Use a large wooden spoon to mix the dough very lightly but well enough so that everything is incorporated.

5. Pinch off bits of dough and form into 1½-inch balls. Arrange 1 inch apart on cookie sheets. These will not spread. Bake 15 to 20 minutes until they start to turn a very light brown.

6. Remove from oven and place cookie sheets on wire racks to cool. While cookies are still warm, roll them in confectioners' sugar. Let cool completely and store in an airtight container.

Yield: about 80 cookies
Will keep: 2 to 3 weeks at room temperature

Good husband and huswife, now chiefly be glad,
things handsome to have, as they ought to be had.
They both do provide, against Christmas do come,
to welcome their neighbors, good chere to have some.
—Thomas Tusser (1573)

• ROLLED ALMOND CHRISTMAS WAFERS •

Mrs. Bobs Strachan, who lives in Minnesota and bakes some of the best cookies I've ever tasted, always includes these charmers in her Christmas baking. The cookies are pressed around the handle of a wooden spoon while they are still warm for lovely flute-shaped cookies. But arm yourself with patience. Making these cookies is time consuming—you will be able to bake only about 4 cookies at one time. The end result, of course, is worth the effort.

⅔ cup blanched almonds, finely
    ground
½ cup sugar
1 stick sweet butter
1 tablespoon all-purpose flour
2 tablespoons milk

½ teaspoon almond extract

Equipment: *a large heavy skillet; cookie sheets, lined with parchment paper* or *lightly greased and floured; wire cooling racks*

1. Preheat oven to 350°F.
2. Place all the ingredients in a heavy skillet.
3. Cook, stirring constantly, over low heat, until the butter is melted and everything is well blended. Keep skillet warm over very low heat or set on a flame tamer while you are working.
4. Drop mixture by teaspoonfuls 4 inches apart on prepared cookie sheets. Bake 5 to 6 minutes, until cookies are lightly browned.
5. Remove from oven and let cool on cookie sheets for a minute or so until

cookies can be lifted with a spatula without sticking. Press each warm cookie around the handle of a wooden spoon for a flutelike shape, then place on wire racks to cool. Store completely cooled cookies in an airtight container.

Yield: about 30 cookies
Will keep: 1 week at room temperature

I do hope your Christmas has had a little touch of Eternity in among the rush and pitter patter and all. It always seems such a mixing of this world and the next—but that after all is the idea!

—Evelyn Underhill

• OATMEAL LACE COOKIES •

This is an extremely easy cookie to make, yet it always creates a small sensation. The cookies are thin, very crisp, and have a lacy transparency. Bake these with a child to demonstrate a special kind of kitchen magic: Little lumps of dough are transformed in the oven into very beautiful and delicious cookies.

1½ cups rolled oats
½ cup all-purpose flour
¾ cup firmly packed dark brown
   sugar
¼ teaspoon baking soda
¼ teaspoon salt
1 stick plus 3 tablespoons sweet
   butter
1 large egg

¼ cup heavy cream
1 teaspoon pure vanilla extract
Optional:
½ cup dried currants, soaked in 2
   tablespoons brandy

Equipment: *electric mixer; cookie
   sheets, lined with parchment paper
   or foil; wire cooling racks*

1. Preheat oven to 350°F.

2. In a large bowl, mix together the oats, flour, sugar, baking soda, and salt.

3. Melt the butter in a small, heavy saucepan over very low heat.

4. In a small bowl beat the egg together with the heavy cream and vanilla extract. Stir in currants if using. Stir in melted butter.

5. Stir the liquid ingredients into the oat-flour mixture and combine well.

Drop by teaspoonfuls onto prepared cookie sheets, leaving at least 3 inches between each cookie. These will thin out and spread.

6. Bake 5 or 6 minutes, until lightly browned. Remove from oven and cool on cookie sheets for several minutes, until cookies hold their shape. Carefully remove with a spatula, and place on a wire rack to cool completely. Store in an airtight container.

Yield: about 4 dozen cookies
Will keep: several weeks at room temperature

• MAPLE WALNUT COOKIES •

These cookies capture all the wonderful flavors of New England, combining the silky sweet flavor of maple syrup with the tang of toasted walnuts. This is a very nice cookie to include as part of a selection of cookies to be mailed as Christmas presents.

¾ cup walnut halves
1 cup all-purpose flour
½ teaspoon baking powder
¼ teaspoon baking soda
1 stick sweet butter
½ cup maple syrup

¼ cup sugar

Equipment: *cookie sheets, lined with parchment paper or foil; 1 large and 1 medium saucepan; wire cooling racks*

1. Preheat oven to 350°F.
2. Spread walnut halves in a single layer on a cookie sheet and toast for 10 to 15 minutes in preheated 350°F oven. Remove and let cool. Rub nuts between your hands to remove any loose skin. Chop coarsely with a large sharp knife.
3. In a small bowl, whisk together flour, baking powder, and baking soda. Set aside.
4. Fill a large saucepan with 3 inches of water and bring to a simmer.
5. In a smaller saucepan, heat butter, maple syrup, and sugar. Bring to a boil and continue boiling until sugar is completely dissolved.
6. Place smaller saucepan into larger saucepan with simmering water and

remove from heat. Stir flour into sugar mixture, then fold in the chopped walnuts.

7. Keep dough warm over hot water. Drop by teaspoonfuls on cookie sheet, leaving 3 inches between each cookie.

8. Bake for 7 minutes, until cookies are slightly firm to the touch. Remove from oven and transfer cookies to wire racks to cool. Store completely cooled cookies in an airtight container.

Yield: 2 dozen cookies
Will keep: 1 month at room temperature

• GINGER SNAPS •

Christmas is the time for recalling old favorites—toys, decorations, books, music, and cookies. For me these ginger snaps, thicker and crunchier than the store-bought kind, are the ultimate comfort food. Good any time of day, dunk these in milk, coffee, tea, or even a glass of wine. They are easy to make, keep a long time, and are excellent for mailing.

2 cups all-purpose flour
1½ teaspoons baking soda
½ teaspoon salt
2 teaspoons ground ginger
1 teaspoon cinnamon
½ teaspoon ground cloves
1 stick sweet butter, softened
1 cup light brown sugar

1 large egg
¼ cup molasses
1 teaspoon white vinegar
Granulated sugar for coating

Equipment: *electric mixer; cookie sheets, lined with parchment paper or foil; wire cooling racks*

1. Preheat oven to 350°F.

2. In a medium bowl, stir flour, baking soda, salt, ground ginger, cinnamon, and ground cloves with a wire whisk, to blend.

3. In a large bowl, cream butter with an electric mixer at medium speed. Increase speed and gradually beat in sugar. Continue beating until mixture is light and fluffy. Beat in egg, molasses, and vinegar. With the mixer at low speed, beat in flour mixture until just incorporated. Scrape dough into a large plastic bag and knead until it is smooth and sticks together.

4. Roll teaspoonfuls of dough into 1-inch balls. Roll balls in granulated sugar and place them 2 inches apart on prepared cookie sheets. Press a crisscross pattern on each cookie with the tines of a fork, but do not flatten the cookies too much. They should be about ½ inch thick.

5. Bake about 15 minutes. Cookies should feel almost firm to the touch. Remove from oven and transfer cookies to wire racks to cool. Store completely cooled cookies in an airtight container.

Yield: 50 to 60 cookies
Will keep: several months at room temperature

And may your happiness ever spread
Like butter on hot gingerbread.
—Anonymous

• ROBYN'S CHOCOLATE "OH"S •

Robyn Low, an extraordinarily talented chef, bakes these cookies for special occasions, for special friends, and for special bribes. (I know she gets better service from shopkeepers and delivery persons because they're hooked on these cookies.) The name becomes self-explanatory when you've tasted one. The only appropriate response is to lift your eyes heavenward and softly exclaim, "Oh!"

These cookies do not keep well, so make them for instant consumption and gratification.

½ cup raisins
Boiling water
2 ounces unsweetened chocolate
8 ounces semisweet chocolate
3 tablespoons sweet butter
¼ cup cake flour
2 teaspoons powdered instant coffee
¼ teaspoon baking powder
¼ teaspoon salt

2 large eggs
½ cup sugar
1 teaspoon pure vanilla extract
1 cup semisweet chocolate chips
½ cup chopped pecans

Equipment: *electric mixer; cookie sheets, lined with parchment paper or foil; wire cooling racks*

1. Preheat oven to 350°F.

2. In a small bowl, pour boiling water over raisins so that they are just covered. Let stand 10 minutes, drain, and set aside.

3. Cut the chocolate into small pieces. Melt butter and chocolate in top of

double boiler set over (but not touching) barely simmering water. When almost melted, remove from heat and stir until mixed and completely melted. Set aside.

4. In a small bowl, stir flour, instant coffee, baking powder, and salt with a wire whisk, to blend.

5. In a large bowl, beat eggs, sugar, and vanilla extract together with an electric mixer, until thick and very pale. Beat in the melted chocolate. At low speed, beat in the flour mixture until just incorporated. With a large spatula, fold in chocolate chips, pecans, and raisins.

6. Drop by teaspoonfuls 2 inches apart on prepared cookie sheets. Work quickly as the dough will stiffen.

7. Bake 8 to 10 minutes, until tops look crackly. Remove from oven and transfer cookies to wire racks to cool. Store completely cooled cookies in an airtight container.

Yield: 2 to 3 dozen cookies
Will keep: 2 days at room temperature

What makes these cookies "grown-up" is the addition of macadamia nuts and the fact that the chips aren't really chips but irregular chunks of the best bittersweet chocolate you can find. If you are feeling only moderately grown-up you can, of course, substitute chocolate chips for the chocolate chunks; and if you are feeling frugal, substitute an equal amount of any other nuts for the macadamias.

1 cup all-purpose flour
½ teaspoon baking soda
½ teaspoon salt (omit if using salted macadamia nuts)
1 stick sweet butter, softened
⅔ cup packed light brown sugar
1 large egg
1 teaspoon pure vanilla extract
6 ounces bittersweet chocolate (preferably Lindt), chopped into small chunks with a knife

¾ cup macadamia nuts, chopped into small chunks with a knife
Granulated sugar for topping

Equipment: *electric mixer; cookie sheets, lined with parchment paper or lightly greased; wire cooling racks*

1. Preheat oven to 375°F.
2. In a small bowl, stir flour, baking soda, and salt with a wire whisk, to blend.
3. In a large bowl, cream butter with an electric mixer at medium speed.

Increase speed and gradually beat in sugar. Continue beating until mixture is light and fluffy. Beat in the egg and vanilla extract. On low speed, beat in flour mixture until just incorporated.

4. With a large wooden spoon, fold in chocolate chunks and chopped macadamia nuts.

5. Drop by teaspoonfuls 2 inches apart onto prepared cookie sheets. Flatten each cookie with the bottom of a glass dipped in granulated sugar. Bake 10 to 12 minutes, until edges turn golden brown. Remove from oven and let cool on cookie sheet for a minute or two. Transfer cookies to a wire rack to cool. Store completely cooled cookies in an airtight container.

Yield: about 3 dozen cookies
Will keep: 1 month at room temperature

Listen, would you like some cookies? I put a small assortment on this plate. Sugar, oatmeal, double fudge, chocolate chip. If there is a different one that you would prefer, ask.

—Bette Pesetsky

◆ THE BEST FUDGY BROWNIES ◆

I was going to omit this recipe on the theory that everyone already has more brownie recipes than they can use. But my husband and nephews, brownie connoisseurs and passionate lovers of all things chocolate, disapproved. In our family there is no holiday without these brownies and Christmas is no exception. The recipe came to me from my friend Winnie Rosen, and I have never changed a single thing in it.

4 ounces unsweetened chocolate
5½ tablespoons sweet butter
2 large eggs
1 cup sugar
½ cup all-purpose flour
¼ teaspoon salt

1 teaspoon vanilla extract
½ cup chopped walnuts

Equipment: electric mixer; greased 9-by-9-inch pan

1. Preheat oven to 350°F.

2. Melt chocolate together with the butter in the top of a double boiler set over (but not touching) barely simmering water. When most of the chocolate has melted, remove top of double boiler from heat and stir until mixed and completely melted. Set aside.

3. In a large bowl, beat eggs and sugar together with an electric mixer at high speed until just foamy, about 30 seconds. Take care not to overbeat the eggs and sugar as this will make the texture of the brownies more cakelike and dry than moist and fudgy. An alternate method is to beat the eggs and

sugar vigorously for up to a minute with a wire whisk. Stir in melted chocolate mixture. Stir in flour, salt, and vanilla extract. Fold in walnuts.

4. Pour mixture into prepared pan. Bake about 20 to 25 minutes. Test by inserting toothpick in center. It should come out clean but not dry. Do not overbake as these should be slightly moist in the center.

5. Remove from oven and cool in pan. Turn out of pan by inverting onto a cutting board. To cut into neat pieces, chill the brownie cake in the freezer for 30 minutes. Cut chilled cake into squares or bars using a long sharp or serrated knife. Store in an airtight container in refrigerator or freezer, or wrap individually and store in refrigerator or freezer.

Yield: about 24 brownies
Will keep: 1 week at room temperature; 1 month refrigerated; several months in the freezer

• CHOCOLATE MADELEINES •

Is it a cake? Is it a cookie? No matter. To my taste, these are even more memorable than the very plain cookie that inspired Marcel Proust to write his monumental novel, *Remembrance of Things Past*. Marcel Proust dipped his madeleines into a cup of lime-flower tea, which is probably very nice, but I prefer a cup of strong coffee. After a few days the cookies get increasingly drier, making them perfect for dunking. These are very pretty cookies that are easy to mail, and they make an extravagant gift when paired with a madeleine mold.

1¼ cups sifted cake flour
2 tablespoons unsweetened Dutch process cocoa
¼ teaspoon salt
1 stick plus 2 tablespoons sweet butter
3 ounces bittersweet chocolate (preferably Lindt), broken up into small pieces
3 large eggs plus 2 eggs yolks
½ cup sugar

1 teaspoon vanilla brandy (page 121)
or
1 teaspoon pure vanilla extract
¼ cup confectioners' sugar, for dusting finished cookies

Equipment: *electric mixer; 3 madeleine molds (3½-by-2-inch shells) sprayed with nonstick cooking spray; wire cooling racks*

1. Preheat oven to 350°F.
2. Sift together flour, cocoa, and salt. Set aside.

set over (but not touching) barely simmering water. When almost melted, remove from heat and stir until mixed and completely melted. Set aside.

4. In a large bowl, beat eggs and egg yolks with an electric mixer at high speed until frothy. Add sugar and vanilla brandy (or extract) and beat until mixture turns pale yellow. Add melted butter and chocolate and mix on low speed to blend. Add flour-cocoa mixture and mix on low speed to blend.

5. Place a rounded tablespoonful of the batter into each madeleine mold. No need to spread it, it will do so when baking. Bake for 10 to 12 minutes, until madeleines spring back when pressed lightly with finger.

6. Remove from oven and slide madeleines out onto wire rack to cool. (If you have only 1 madeleine mold: bake the madeleines, remove from mold, let mold cool, spray again, fill, and bake. Repeat for third batch.) When madeleines are completely cool, store between layers of wax paper in an airtight container. Dust madeleines with confectioners' sugar before serving.

Yield: 36 madeleines
Will keep: 2 weeks at room temperature

• CHOCO-COCO KISSES •

These cookies look particularly nice when piped through a pastry bag (see page 17). You can also drop the batter by teaspoonfuls onto the cookie sheet. These won't be beautiful but they will still be delicious. For a truly spectacular cookie, dip half of each cookie in a chocolate glaze after the cookies have baked and cooled.

2 egg whites at room temperature
½ teaspoon vanilla extract
¼ teaspoon salt
½ cup superfine sugar
or
½ cup granulated sugar, processed in a food processor with a metal blade until the texture of the sugar becomes very fine
1 cup flaked, unsweetened coconut (can be found in health food stores)

½ cup semisweet mini chocolate chips

Equipment: *pastry bag with #6 (½-inch-diameter) pastry tube or gallon size plastic reclosable freezer bag with #6 (½-inch-diameter) pastry tube (both optional); cookie sheets, nonstick or lined with baking parchment or foil; wire cooling racks*

1. Preheat oven to 325°F.
2. In a large bowl, beat egg whites, vanilla extract, and salt with an electric mixer at high speed until soft peaks form. Add sugar gradually and continue beating until stiff peaks form.
3. Fold in coconut and chocolate chips.

tube slightly above cookie sheet. Squeeze out meringue, gradually raising the tube as meringue begins to build, but keeping the tip buried in the meringue. When you have piped out a 1½-to-2-inch round, stop squeezing and raise tip to make a point. The meringues should look like large kisses. Continue piping the meringues 1 inch apart. Don't worry if the shapes are not perfect or if the sizes vary. It will make no difference to the taste. As you practice you will get the hang of it, and might even come up with your own preferred method and shape.

5. Bake 20 minutes, until cookies are firm and just beginning to brown. Remove from oven and let cool on cookie sheet for a minute or two. Transfer cookies to wire racks to cool. Store completely cooled cookies in an airtight container.

Yield: 2 dozen cookies
Will keep: 2 months at room temperature

CHOCOLATE DIPPING GLAZE

4 ounces bittersweet or semisweet chocolate

1 tablespoon sweet butter

1. Break or cut chocolate into small pieces. Melt chocolate together with 1 tablespoon sweet butter in the top of a double boiler set over (but not touching) barely simmering water. When most of the chocolate has melted, remove from heat and stir until it has all melted.

2. Dip the pointy top of each completely cooled cookie into the chocolate and dry on wire rack.

• CHOCOLATE HAZELNUT MACAROONS •

What is a macaroon? It can be a crunchy almond cookie; a chewy coconut confection; or a divine combination of hazelnuts and chocolate suspended in a meringue, as in the following recipe. The ease with which these cookies are put together belie their sophisticated crunch and flavor. Serve them on their own or with an assortment of other cookies.

1 cup toasted hazelnuts
2 ounces unsweetened chocolate,
  chopped into small pieces
¾ cup sugar
3 egg whites at room temperature
¼ teaspoon cream of tartar
Pinch of salt
½ teaspoon pure vanilla extract

Equipment: *food processor; electric mixer; pastry bag fitted with #6 (½-inch-diameter) pastry tube or gallon-size reclosable plastic freezer bag with #6 (½-inch-diameter) pastry tube (both optional); cookie sheets, lined with parchment paper or foil; wire cooling racks*

1. Preheat oven to 350°F.

2. Spread hazelnuts in a baking pan, and toast for 10 to 15 minutes in preheated oven. Remove and let cool a little. As soon as they are cool enough to handle, rub nuts between your hands to loosen and remove as much of their brown skins as possible.

3. When hazelnuts are completely cool, grind them, together with the chocolate and ¼ cup sugar, in a food processor to a fine powder.

4. In a large bowl, beat the egg whites, cream of tartar, and salt with an electric mixer at medium speed until soft peaks form. Gradually beat in the

remaining sugar and the vanilla extract; increase speed to high, and beat until stiff peaks form.

5. Fold in ground chocolate and hazelnut mixture. Fill pastry or freezer bag with meringue mixture. Hold bag upright over prepared cookie sheet and squeeze out meringue, leaving pastry tip buried in the meringue, until you have piped out a round about 1½ inches in diameter. Lift up tip and stop squeezing. You will have a pretty kiss-shaped cookie. Leave 1 inch between each cookie. Alternately, drop meringue mixture from a tablespoon on prepared cookie sheets, leaving a 2-inch space between each cookie.

6. Bake 15 to 20 minutes. Remove from oven and cool for a few minutes before transferring cookies to a wire rack. Cool completely and store in an airtight container.

Yield: about 2 dozen macaroons
Will keep: 1 month at room temperature

• COFFEE MERINGUE KISSES •

This is a very grown-up cookie with a long and illustrious history. It is said that Marie Antoinette loved meringue kisses so much that she was given to rolling up her royal sleeves and whipping up the meringues with her own royal hands. If you leave out the coffee and vanilla flavoring you will have perfectly white meringue kisses, meltingly pure and simple in taste. But I prefer the more sophisticated version set out here. They are delicious, 100% fat-free, about 20 calories per cookie, and a great gift for anyone with wheat allergies.

These cookies are prettier if you pipe them through a pastry bag, but lacking one you can drop the meringue mixture from a tablespoon onto the prepared cookie sheet.

¾ cup sugar
3 teaspoons powdered instant coffee
* or espresso*
4 egg whites (measuring
* 1 liquid cup) at room*
* temperature*
1 teaspoon vanilla
* extract*
¼ teaspoon cream of tartar

Equipment: *food processor; electric mixer; cookie sheets, with a non-stick surface* or *lined with parchment paper; pastry bag fitted with #6 (½-inch-diameter) plain round pastry tube* or *a gallon-size reclosable freezer bag with #6 (½-inch-diameter) pastry tube (both optional); wire cooling racks*

1. Preheat oven to 250°F.
2. In a food processor with a metal blade, process the sugar and coffee powder for several minutes until the texture of the sugar becomes very fine.

3. In a large mixing bowl, beat the egg whites and vanilla extract with an electric mixer at medium speed, until very frothy. Add cream of tartar, and continue beating at medium speed until soft peaks form. Increase beater speed to high, and gradually beat in the sugar-coffee mixture. Continue beating until stiff peaks form and mixture has a glossy sheen.

4. Fill pastry or freezer bag with meringue. Hold bag upright over prepared cookie sheet and squeeze out meringue, leaving pastry tip buried in the meringue, until you have piped out a round about 1½ inches in diameter. Lift up tip and stop squeezing. You will have a pretty kiss-shaped cookie. Leave 1 inch between each cookie. Alternately, drop meringue mixture from a tablespoon on prepared cookie sheets, leaving a 2-inch space between each cookie.

5. Bake 1 hour *without opening oven door*. Turn off oven, and let meringues dry in oven for 2 to 3 hours longer without opening oven door. (After the first hour, okay to peek just once.) At this point you can leave them in the oven overnight.

6. Remove baked meringues from cookie sheet with a spatula. Store in an airtight container.

Yield: about 3 dozen cookies
Will keep: several months at room temperature

• RASPBERRY LINZER HEARTS •

Although these cookies seem perfect for Valentine's Day, they are too pretty and too delicious to leave out of a Christmas cookie collection. I always make them for Christmas, but then I usually make them for every other festive occasion as well.

2 cups toasted hazelnuts
¾ cup sugar
1½ cups all-purpose flour
½ teaspoon ground cinnamon
Grated rind of 1 lemon
1 stick plus 2 tablespoons sweet
butter, refrigerator cold
1 large egg, lightly beaten
½ cup seedless raspberry jam

Vanilla confectioners' sugar (page 123)

Equipment: *food processor; 2½-inch heart-shaped cookie cutter, a smaller heart-shaped cookie cutter or heart-shaped aspic cutter; cookie sheets, lined with parchment paper or ungreased; wire cooling racks*

1. Preheat oven to 350°F.

2. Grind hazelnuts and ¼ cup of the sugar in a food processor with a metal blade until finely ground. Remove mixture and set aside.

3. Process remaining sugar in a food processor with a metal blade until sugar is very fine. Add flour, cinnamon, and lemon rind and process to mix. With motor on, add butter in small pieces and process until the mixture resembles coarse meal.

4. Transfer to a large bowl. Add hazelnut mixture and egg and stir with a spatula or wooden spoon until mixture is well blended. Scrape out onto lightly floured surface and knead gently until mixture sticks together.

5. Divide dough in half. Wrap and refrigerate one half while you work with the other. Roll out dough to a thickness of ¼ inch. Cut out cookies with larger heart-shaped cookie cutter. Use the smaller cookie cutter to remove centers from half of the cookie hearts. Transfer large hearts, heart frames, and the tiny hearts to prepared cookie sheets.

6. Bake 8 to 10 minutes, until they are very lightly colored. Remove from oven and transfer cookies to wire racks to cool.

7. When cookies have cooled completely, spread jam on all the larger hearts. Sift vanilla confectioners' sugar onto the heart frames. Place heart frames on jam-covered hearts. Dust the tiny hearts with confectioners' sugar.

Yield: 2 dozen filled cookies and lots of little heart centers
Will keep: The cookies will keep for several weeks in an airtight container before they are assembled. Once you have assembled the jam-filled sandwiches they should be consumed within a week.

• JAM-FILLED THIMBLE COOKIES •

This cookie is an old-fashioned classic, always popular and extremely pretty. Use your favorite red jam or strained preserves. Incidentally, if you've lost your thimble or simply don't have one, use your thumb to indent the cookies. These would then be called "Thumb-Print Cookies."

1½ cups all-purpose flour
¼ teaspoon salt
⅓ cup sugar
1 stick plus 3 tablespoons sweet butter
2 egg yolks
1 teaspoon vanilla extract
2 egg whites, lightly beaten

¾ cup (6 ounces) finely chopped, toasted walnuts or pecans
Approximately ½ cup red jam or strained preserves

Equipment: *food processor* or *electric mixer; thimble; cookie sheets, lined with parchment paper* or *lightly greased; wire cooling racks*

1. Preheat oven to 350°F.
2. In a small bowl, stir flour and salt with a wire whisk, to blend. Set aside.
3. In a food processor with a metal blade, process the sugar for several minutes until the texture of the sugar becomes very fine. With the processor on, add the butter in small pieces and process until smooth and creamy. Scrape down sides of bowl, add egg yolks and vanilla extract, and process until completely incorporated. Scrape down sides of bowl again; add flour mixture gradually, and process to incorporate each addition before adding more flour, until all the flour has been incorporated.

4. Shape rounded tablespoonfuls into balls. Dip each ball into egg whites, then roll in finely chopped nuts. Place 1 inch apart on prepared cookie sheets. With a thimble, make an indentation in the center of each cookie.

5. Bake for 15 to 20 minutes until cookies are slightly browned around the edges. Remove from oven and transfer cookies to wire racks to cool. When cookies are completely cool, fill with your favorite jam or preserves. Store in an airtight container, with several sheets of wax paper between each layer of cookies.

Yield: about 3 dozen cookies
Will keep: about 2 weeks at room temperature

Using an electric mixer: Remove butter from refrigerator 30 minutes before using, to soften. In a large bowl, cream butter with an electric mixer at medium speed. Increase speed and gradually beat in sugar. Continue beating until mixture is light and fluffy. Beat in egg yolks and vanilla extract. On low speed, beat in flour mixture until just incorporated.

• ORANGE-ALMOND TUILES •

These cookies are said to resemble the tiles (*tuiles* in French) on the roofs of country cottages. The unique thing about these cookies is that they are draped over a rolling pin while they are still warm and soft, so that they cool to a rounded shape. A rolling pin, however, holds only a few cookies at a time, so I pass on to you a trick I learned from a friend—drape your cookies over a broomstick handle suspended between two chairs. I should also tell you that if you are feeling lazy and want to leave the cookies flat, they will be just as delicious and, in fact, much easier to store.

5 tablespoons sweet butter, softened
⅓ cup confectioners' sugar
1 egg white, unbeaten
1 tablespoon Grand Marnier
1 tablespoon orange zest
⅓ cup all-purpose flour

⅓ cup slivered almonds

Equipment: *electric mixer; cookie sheets, lined with parchment paper or tin foil; broom handle or rolling pin; wire cooling racks*

1. Preheat oven to 400°F.
2. In a medium-size bowl, cream together the butter and sugar with an electric mixer at high speed, until mixture is light and fluffy. Beat in the egg white, Grand Marnier, and orange zest. Use a large wooden spoon or rubber spatula to stir in the flour and almonds.
3. Drop by teaspoonfuls at least 3 inches apart on prepared cookie sheets. Dip the tines of a fork in cold water and flatten tops of cookies.
4. Bake for 6 to 8 minutes or until the edges start to brown. Slide cookies

off cookie sheet with a spatula and drape over a broomstick handle or rolling pin. Let cool completely. Store *tuiles* very carefully between layers of wax paper in an airtight container. These cookies are very fragile and are best eaten quickly.

Yield: 2 dozen tuiles
Will keep: 1 week at room temperature

There is nothing sadder in this world than to awake Christmas morning and not be a child . . . . Time, self-pity, apathy, bitterness, and exhaustion can take the Christmas out of the child, but you cannot take the child out of Christmas.

—Erma Bombeck

· CHRISTMAS OATMEAL COOKIES ·

This is a wonderful oatmeal cookie, soft and chewy, and much enlivened by the addition of bananas and dried cranberries. They keep extremely well (for as long as a month) and are very good cookies for mailing.

1½ cups flour
1 teaspoon baking soda
1 teaspoon baking powder
¼ teaspoon salt
2 sticks sweet butter, softened
¾ cup sugar
¾ cup brown sugar
2 large eggs
2 ripe bananas, mashed
1 teaspoon vanilla extract

3 cups rolled oats
1 cup dried cranberries
Topping:
Additional granulated sugar

Equipment: *electric mixer or food processor; cookie sheets, lined with parchment paper or foil; wire cooling racks*

1. Preheat oven to 350°F.

2. In a small bowl, stir flour, baking soda, baking powder, and salt with a wire whisk, to blend. Set aside.

3. In a large bowl, cream the butter with an electric mixer at medium speed. Raise speed to high and gradually beat in granulated sugar, then brown sugar. Continue beating until mixture is light and fluffy. Beat in eggs, one at a time, until completely incorporated. Beat in the mashed bananas and vanilla extract. Scrape down sides of bowl when necessary. Reduce beater speed to low, and gradually beat in flour mixture. Use a large wooden spoon to stir in rolled oats and dried cranberries.

4. Drop by tablespoonfuls to make golf-size balls, 2 inches apart, on prepared cookie sheet. Flatten each cookie with the bottom of a water glass that has been dipped in sugar.

5. Bake 10 to 12 minutes until cookies are golden brown. Tops should feel springy when lightly touched. Slide parchment paper or foil off cookie sheets and let cool for a few minutes. Transfer cookies to wire racks to cool. Store completely cooled cookies in an airtight container.

Yield: about 4 dozen cookies
Will keep: 1 month at room temperature

Using a food processor: With a metal blade, process both sugars for several minutes until the texture of the sugar becomes very fine. With the processor on, add the butter in small pieces and process until smooth and creamy. Scrape down sides of bowl; add eggs, and process until eggs are completely incorporated. Scrape down sides of bowl; add bananas and vanilla extract, and process until completely incorporated. Scrape down sides of bowl again, add flour mixture gradually, and process to incorporate each addition before adding more flour, until all the flour has been incorporated. Scrape mixture out of food processor bowl into a large mixing bowl. Use a large wooden spoon to stir in rolled oats and dried cranberries.

• OATMEAL, RAISIN, CRANBERRY, PECAN, CHOCOLATE CHIP COOKIES •

A friend in Eugene, Oregon, sent me this recipe with a note saying, "As far as I can tell, this cookie includes every major food group, at least the ones that are important to me. I wouldn't dream of going on a hike, a bike ride, or even an extended trip to the mall without taking a few of these along to sustain and revive me." It is, indeed, an excellent cookie for every occasion.

1 cup raisins
1 cup dried cranberries
Boiling water
1½ cups all-purpose flour
1 teaspoon baking soda
½ teaspoon salt
2 sticks sweet butter, softened
⅔ cup granulated sugar
⅔ cup packed brown sugar
2 teaspoons vanilla extract

2 large eggs
2 cups rolled oats
1 cup chocolate chips
1 cup pecans, coarsely chopped
Additional granulated sugar

Equipment: *electric mixer; cookie sheets, lined with parchment paper or lightly greased; wire racks for cooling*

1. Preheat oven to 375°F.

2. In a small bowl, combine raisins and cranberries. Pour in boiling water just to cover. Let stand for 10 minutes. Drain in a strainer and set aside.

3. In another bowl, stir flour, baking soda, and salt with a wire whisk, to blend. Set aside.

4. In a large bowl, cream butter with an electric mixer at medium speed.

Increase speed and gradually beat in granulated sugar, followed by brown sugar and vanilla extract. Continue beating until mixture is light and fluffy. Keeping the mixer at high speed, beat in the eggs one at a time.

5. Reduce speed and gradually mix in flour mixture.

6. Use a large wooden spoon to fold in the rolled oats. Fold in the chocolate chips, the pecans, and the raisins and cranberries.

7. Drop by teaspoonfuls 2 inches apart onto prepared cookie sheets. Pour some granulated sugar in a small bowl. Wet the bottom of a water glass, dip in granulated sugar, and press each cookie gently to flatten the top. Dip bottom of glass in granulated sugar before pressing each cookie.

8. Bake cookies 10 to 12 minutes, until cookies are golden brown. Remove from oven, let cool on cookie sheets for a few minutes, then transfer cookies to wire racks to cool. Store completely cooled cookies in an airtight container.

Yield: 3 to 4 dozen cookies
Will keep: several weeks at room temperature

· WALNUT KISSES ·

This is a quick and easy cookie to bake and makes a nice addition to an assortment of Christmas cookies served during the holidays or sent to special friends. A lovely extra is to paint these cookies with either a milk glaze (page 78) or a lemon glaze (page 93).

*1¼ cups (5 ounces) walnut halves
and pieces*
1 large egg
*1 cup vanilla sugar (page 122), or
substitute 1 cup sugar plus 1
teaspoon vanilla extract*
⅓ cup flour

Optional topping:
Milk glaze (page 78)
or
Lemon glaze (page 93)

Equipment: *electric mixer; cookie
sheets, lined with parchment paper
or lightly greased; wire cooling
racks*

1. Preheat oven to 375°F.
2. Spread the walnuts in a single layer in a shallow baking pan. Bake for 10 to 12 minutes or until nuts are almost too hot to touch. Remove from oven and let cool. Break them into largish pieces with your hands and set aside. It doesn't matter that the nuts are not all the same size.
3. In a large bowl, beat the egg with an electric mixer at medium speed until it is very thick and light in color. Continue beating while gradually adding the sugar. Increase speed to high and beat until mixture turns a pale color and forms a ribbon.

4. Use a rubber spatula to fold in the flour and walnuts. Blend together very gently.

5. Drop by half teaspoonfuls in little mounds on prepared cookie sheets and bake for 10 minutes, until cookies are just firm and starting to turn a golden brown. Remove from oven and transfer cookies to wire racks to cool. When cookies are completely cool, you may paint them with either of the glazes listed above. Let dry completely. Store cookies in an airtight container.

Yield: 3 dozen cookies
Will keep: several weeks

• CARAWAY SEED COOKIES •

Not too sweet and very fragrant with the spicy scent of caraway seeds, these are delicious cookies to serve with afternoon tea or for a snack anytime.

2 cups all-purpose flour
1 cup whole wheat flour
2 teaspoons baking powder
3 teaspoons caraway seeds
½ teaspoon salt
2 sticks sweet butter, softened
¾ cup sugar

2 large eggs
¼ cup water

Equipment: electric mixer; cookie sheets, lined with parchment paper or lightly greased; wire cooling racks

1. Preheat oven to 350°F.
2. In a large bowl, whisk together both flours, baking powder, caraway seeds, and salt. Set aside.
3. In a large bowl, cream butter with an electric mixer at medium speed. Increase speed and gradually beat in sugar. Continue beating until mixture is light and fluffy. Beat in eggs, one at a time, and water. On low speed, beat in flour mixture until just incorporated.
4. Gather the dough into a ball and remove to a lightly floured surface. Divide dough in half and roll out, one half at a time, to ⅛-inch thickness. Cut into rounds with a 3-inch cookie cutter and place on prepared cookie sheets.
5. Bake 10 to 12 minutes, until edges are slightly browned. Remove from oven and transfer cookies to wire racks to cool. Store completely cooled

cookies in an airtight container. The flavor of these cookies improves after 3 or 4 days.

Yield: about 3 dozen cookies
Will keep: 1 month at room temperature

I can understand people simply fleeing the mountainous effort Christmas has become . . . . But there are always a few saving graces and finally they make up for all the bother and distress.

—May Sarton

• VANILLA WAFERS •

These are simple, old-fashioned cookies for the pure of heart and palate. They are also a necessary ingredient in the more sinfully inclined Bourbon Balls (page 111).

1 cup sugar
1½ sticks sweet butter
¼ teaspoon salt
3 egg whites
2 teaspoons pure vanilla extract
1⅓ cups cake flour

Equipment: *food processor; cookie sheets, lined with parchment paper or lightly greased; wire cooling racks*

1. Preheat oven to 375°F.

2. In a food processor with a metal blade, process the sugar for several minutes until the texture of the sugar becomes very fine. With the processor on, add the butter in small pieces and process until smooth and creamy. Add the salt, egg whites, and vanilla extract. Process until incorporated. Scrape down sides of bowl; add flour, and pulse until just blended.

3. Drop cookie batter by teaspoonfuls 3 inches apart on prepared cookie sheets. Try to keep them neat, rounded, and the same size.

4. Bake 10 to 12 minutes, until edges turn light brown but centers are pale. Remove from oven and transfer cookies to wire racks to cool. Store completely cooled cookies in an airtight container.

Yield: about 4 dozen
Will keep: 1 month at room temperature

Using an electric mixer: Remove butter from refrigerator 30 minutes before using to soften. In a large bowl, cream butter with an electric mixer at medium speed. Increase speed and gradually beat in sugar. Continue beating until mixture is light and fluffy. Beat in salt, egg whites, and vanilla extract. On low speed, beat in flour until just incorporated.

Hath not old custom
made this life more sweet?
—William Shakespeare

Jewish almond bread ("mandel" meaning *almond*; "bröt" meaning *bread*) is very similar to the Italian almond biscotti. Both are baked twice to achieve the desired dry, almost brittle texture. Both are only slightly sweet and are the perfect dunking cookie—in coffee, tea, or, as the Italians do it, in a glass of vin santo.

My favorite version, which I learned a long time ago from my anthropology professor, Sula Benet, is flavored with cinnamon. In other versions the cinnamon is replaced by 1 tablespoon grated orange or lemon peel.

3 cups all-purpose flour
2 teaspoons ground cinnamon
1 tablespoon baking powder
¼ teaspoon salt
4 large eggs
1 cup sugar
½ cup flavorless vegetable oil
   (canola or corn)
1 teaspoon almond extract
1 teaspoon vanilla extract

2 cups coarsely chopped unblanched
   almonds
Topping:
1 egg white
2 tablespoons sugar
½ teaspoon cinnamon

Equipment: *electric mixer; cookie sheet, lined with parchment paper or lightly greased*

1. Preheat oven to 350°F.

2. In a medium bowl, stir flour, cinnamon, baking powder, and salt with a whisk, to blend.

3. In a large bowl, beat the eggs and sugar with an electric mixer, until

very light and thick. Beat in the oil, almond extract, and vanilla extract. At low speed, gradually beat in the flour mixture. Using a large wooden spoon, fold in chopped nuts.

4. Remove the dough to a lightly floured surface and knead briefly. Add a little more flour if the dough is sticky. Texture should be soft but not sticky. Shape into 2 logs, each 2 inches in diameter. Beat the egg white lightly with a fork. Mix together sugar and cinnamon. Brush each log with egg white and sprinkle with cinnamon sugar.

5. Bake for 30 to 40 minutes, until logs turn golden brown on the top and become firm. The dough will have spread so that logs are flat on the bottom and curved on top.

6. Remove from oven and place cookie sheets on wire racks to cool. Do not turn off the oven. When almond bread is cool enough to handle but still warm, cut each log into ½-inch slices with a sharp, serrated knife. Place the pieces, cut side down, back on the cookie sheet and bake for 5 minutes. The almond bread pieces should be toasted a golden brown. Leave them in a minute or two longer to achieve this color. Turn the pieces over and bake for another 5 minutes or until golden brown. Remove cookies from cookie sheet and cool on wire racks. Store completely cooled cookies in an airtight container.

Yield: about 3 dozen
Will keep: several months at room temperature

Note: These cookies are also delicious after the first baking, especially if they are served still warm from the oven. They have an appealing soft texture and are quite different from the crisp cookies described above. You can, of course, have the best of both worlds—have some mandelbröt while it is soft and warm, and bake the rest following instructions above. You can rebake them as late as the following day. The crisp, dry cookies will keep much longer than the soft variety.

Two-Step Cookies

These cookies are prepared in two sessions. The dough is mixed and refrigerated, or shaped and allowed to stand overnight to dry. The baking takes place after 2 to 12 hours.

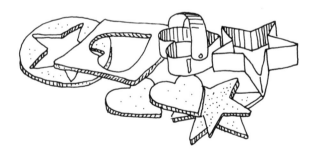

• OLD-FASHIONED SUGAR COOKIES •

These are the classic American sugar cookies. If you make only one type of cookie at Christmastime, this should probably be it. With this one dough you can roll and cut, paint and decorate to your heart's content. It is because of this dough that I can never have enough cookie cutters, and my collection grows and grows every year. Can one ever really have enough angels or Christmas trees, or adorable pigs, stars, or little boys and girls? A tin of these cookies and a set of unusual cookie cutters make a great gift. All sugar cookies are good for mailing.

Bring out your favorite cookie cutters. Assemble all your decorating ingredients—egg yolk paints, glazes, colored sugars, gold and silver dragées, and even gold petal dust. Gather up a multitude of ribbons to turn these cookies into Christmas tree ornaments. This recipe is for a large quantity so that you can eat some, hang some, and give some away as Christmas presents.

4 cups all-purpose flour
2½ teaspoons baking powder
½ teaspoon salt
2 sticks sweet butter, softened
1½ cups superfine sugar (or granulated sugar processed in a food processor with a metal blade until the texture of the sugar becomes very fine)

2 large eggs
4 tablespoons milk
2 teaspoons vanilla extract

Equipment: electric mixer; well-floured pastry cloth; rolling pin; Christmas cookie cutters; cookie sheets, lined with parchment paper or ungreased; wire cooling racks

For decorating: *You will want to have any or all of the following: small- and medium-size brushes; liquid or paste food coloring; gold petal dust; edible glitter in* *an assortment of colors; sparkling sugar; gold and silver dragées, raisins, currants, cinnamon red-hots, mini chocolate chips.*

1. In a large bowl, stir flour, baking powder, and salt with a wire whisk, to blend.

2. In a large bowl, cream the butter with an electric mixer at medium speed. Raise speed to high and gradually beat in the sugar. Continue beating until mixture is light and fluffy. Beat in eggs, one at a time, until completely incorporated. Beat in the milk and vanilla extract.

3. Turn mixer speed to low and gradually beat in the flour mixture. Scrape down the sides of the bowl as necessary with a rubber spatula. Divide dough into 3 parts. Wrap each part in plastic wrap, flatten into a large disk, and refrigerate for 2 hours or overnight.

4. Preheat oven to 350°F.

5. Place one portion of dough on a lightly floured pastry cloth and roll out the dough to desired thickness, from anywhere between ⅛ and ¼ inch (thinner cookies are crispier, thicker cookies are softer and chewier). Cut out shapes with your favorite cookie cutters. Use a spatula to transfer cut-out cookies to prepared cookie sheets. Unbaked cookies may be painted with egg yolk paint (recipe follows) or sprinkled with colored sugar or edible glitter. Gold and silver dragées, decorative candies, raisins, or chocolate chips may be pressed into the unbaked dough. If you are planning to hang the cookies as Christmas tree decorations, make small holes with the blunt end of a wooden skewer or with a plastic straw.

6. Bake for 10 to 12 minutes, until cookies are lightly browned around the edges. Remove from oven and transfer cookies to wire racks to cool. Let cookies cool completely before decorating with milk glaze or gold leaf paint (recipes follow). Store completely cooled cookies in an airtight container.

Yield: 5 to 6 dozen cookies, depending on size
Will keep: several months at room temperature

EGG YOLK PAINT

Egg yolk paint, also called "edible tempera color," is painted onto shaped and cut cookies *before* they are baked. For best success, keep color combinations simple—no more than two colors per cookie. As my freehand painting skills are totally nonexistent, I use cookie presses, cookie cutters, and tiny aspic cutters to lightly press a stencil design in the cookie dough. For example, I press a star or heart shape inside a round cookie. The inside shape gets painted one color, the outside another.

3 to 4 large egg yolks
1 tablespoon water

Paste or *liquid food coloring in*
assorted colors

Equipment: *small bowls or*
custard cups (for as many colors
as you will use but 5 maximum);

small paint brushes; cookie presses
and/or cookie cutters to press designs
into cookies

1. In a small bowl, combine egg yolks and water; beat well with a wire whisk or fork. Divide equally among the bowls.
2. Add food coloring to each bowl, enough to get a color you like.

3. Cover bowls with plastic wrap until ready to use. If the egg yolk paint gets too thick, mix in a few drops of water.

LIQUID GOLD PAINT

You can apply this paint before or after baking.

¼ teaspoon gold petal dust
½ teaspoon vodka (or any other
  clear, high-proof drinking
  alcohol)

Mix gold petal dust and vodka together in a small bowl. Try a little on a sample of dough. Add more gold dust for deeper color.

MILK GLAZE

2 cups confectioners' sugar
3 tablespoons hot milk

2 teaspoons vanilla extract

1. Press confectioners' sugar through a strainer to remove lumps.
2. In a medium-size bowl, combine confectioners' sugar, hot milk, and vanilla extract and beat with a small wire whisk or a fork until well blended and smooth.
3. Cover with plastic wrap until ready to use.

Yield: about ⅔ cup

Note: Here are some of my favorite designs for Christmas Sugar Cookies. They can all be used as Christmas tree ornaments:

1. Cut out angels with an angel-shaped cookie cutter. Punch a hole in the head of the angel before baking. Bake. Paint the body of the angel with white milk glaze; paint the wings with liquid gold paint. Paint a gold halo around the top of the head. Let dry and thread a gold ribbon through the head.
2. Cut out small boys and girls. Paint on colorful costumes with egg yolk paint. Bake.
3. Cut out bears. Press in mini chocolate chips or currants for eyes, nose, and buttons. Punch out a hole. Bake.
4. Cut out stars and Christmas trees. Sprinkle with colored sugars and edible glitter. Bake.

• SPRINGERLE COOKIES •

These venerable cookies, originally thought to be from Germany, are popular Christmas cookies all over Northern Europe. These cookies, in fact, predate Christmas and go back to a time when sacrifices were made to propitiate ancient gods, thereby ensuring the return of the sun. Gradually, cookies baked in animal shapes replaced the sacrifice of real animals. Much later, this tradition evolved into one in which a plate of cookies is left out at night for St. Nicholas, who might be dropping by to leave presents.

Springerle cookies can be among the most beautiful of all Christmas cookies when they are imprinted with a traditional springerle mold or rolling pin. Hand-carved wooden springerle molds from Europe are truly beautiful collector's items, and if it doesn't break your heart to part with one, it makes a truly lavish gift along with a tin of lovely cookies.

The finished cookies can be painted with edible gold paint for a beautiful sheen.

4 to 6 tablespoons anise seeds
4 cups all-purpose flour, plus ½
  cup additional if needed
1 teaspoon baking soda
¼ teaspoon salt
4 large eggs
2 cups sugar
1 teaspoon anise extract
Grated rind of 1 lemon

Optional topping:
Liquid gold paint (page 82)

Equipment: *electric mixer; springerle mold or rolling pin; cookie sheets, lined with parchment paper or lightly greased; wire cooling racks*

1. Sprinkle 1 tablespoon of the anise seeds on each cookie sheet and set aside.

2. In a large bowl, stir flour, baking soda, and salt with a wire whisk, to blend. Set aside.

3. In another large bowl, beat the eggs with an electric mixer at high speed until light and fluffy. Gradually, beat in sugar and continue beating at high speed until mixture is thick and pale. On low speed, beat in anise extract and grated lemon rind. Gradually, beat in flour mixture until just blended. The dough should be smooth, not sticky, and soft enough to roll out. If additional flour is needed to achieve this consistency, beat it in a little at a time until texture is right.

4. Scrape out dough onto a lightly floured surface. Roll it out approximately ⅓ inch thick. Dust springerle mold or rolling pin with flour and shake excess away. Lightly dust rolled-out dough with flour. Press springerle mold or rolling pin into the dough, using strong pressure to form a good impression. Cut between the designs with a sharp knife dipped in flour or a floured pastry wheel. Transfer to prepared cookie sheets. Let cookies stand, uncovered, in a dry place at room temperature for 8 to 12 hours to dry out. If you are going to paint the cookies with liquid gold paint, do so after they have dried and before baking.

5. Preheat oven to 350°F.

6. Place cookies in oven and lower the temperature to 300°F. Bake for 20 to 25 minutes. The cookies should turn a light golden color around the edges, and the unpainted portions of the raised tops should be a pale white.

7. Remove from oven and transfer cookies to wire racks to cool. Store completely cooled cookies between layers of wax paper in a tightly covered

container. Springerle cookies should age several weeks before eating, although they are quite good when they are freshly baked.

Yield: about 60 cookies
Will keep: many months at room temperature

LIQUID GOLD PAINT

¼ teaspoon gold petal dust★
½ teaspoon vodka (or any other clear, high-proof drinking alcohol)

Mix gold petal dust and vodka together in a small bowl. Try a little on a sample of dough. Add more gold dust for deeper color.

★Gold petal dust is available from:
Maid of Scandinavia
3244 Raleigh Avenue
Minneapolis, Minnesota 55416
(800) 328–6722
and

Chocolate Gallery
34 West 22 Street
New York, New York 10010
(212) 675–2253

• A GINGERBREAD MENAGERIE •

Gingerbread boys and girls, and an assortment of animals ranging from dinosaurs and elephants to turtles and ducks, all belong in the household at Christmastime. A large gingerbread cookie, all decked out in holiday finery made up of icing, raisins, and candy, makes a nice stocking stuffer or tie-on tag to another present. Naturally, a few of these charming figures should hang on every well-dressed tree.

These are very good cookies to bake with children—the dough is very manageable and easy to roll out and cut.

3 cups all-purpose flour
1 teaspoon baking soda
¼ teaspoon salt
2½ teaspoons ground ginger
1 teaspoon ground cinnamon
½ teaspoon ground cardamom
½ teaspoon ground nutmeg
¼ teaspoon ground allspice
1½ sticks sweet butter, softened
1 cup firmly packed dark brown
   sugar
½ cup molasses
1 large egg

Equipment: *electric mixer; floured pastry cloth and rolling pin; gingerbread- and animal-shaped cookie cutters; cookie sheets, lined with parchment paper or lightly greased; wire cooling racks*

For decorating: *You can use any or all of the following: royal icing (recipe follows) for piping and/or milk glaze (page 78) for painting; food coloring for icing or glaze; raisins, currants, cinnamon red-hots, and gold and silver dragées for eyes, buttons, etc.*

1. In a large bowl, sift together the flour, baking soda, salt, and spices. Whisk sifted ingredients together to blend well. Set aside.

2. In a large bowl, cream butter with an electric mixer at medium speed. Increase speed and gradually beat in brown sugar. Continue beating until mixture is light and fluffy. Beat in the molasses and egg. At low speed, beat in the flour mixture until just incorporated.

3. Scrape out the dough and divide into two equal parts. Flatten each portion of dough into a disk; wrap it well, and refrigerate for 2 hours or overnight.

4. Preheat oven to 350°F.

5. Roll out dough on a floured pastry cloth or lightly floured surface. Roll out dough ⅛ inch thick for crisp, thin gingerbread; ¼ inch thick for softer, chewier gingerbread. Cut out shapes with gingerbread- or animal-shaped cookie cutters. Traditionally these cookies are rather large, but any size you like is fine. I make large boys and girls and smallish animals. Bake large cookies and small cookies on separate sheets, as they will require different baking times. Transfer cut-out cookies to prepared baking sheets with a large spatula. Make holes for hanging with the blunt end of a wooden skewer or a plastic straw. Press in raisins, candies, or dragées for eyes, buttons, etc., if you wish.

6. Bake 8 to 10 minutes for small cookies, 10 to 12 minutes for large ones. Cookies should be firm to the touch and just beginning to color around the edges. Remove from oven and transfer cookies to wire racks to cool. While cookies are still warm, check the holes to ensure they have not closed. If necessary, puncture again with wooden skewer or plastic straw. Let cool

completely before decorating. Let decorated cookies dry completely; store in an airtight container or hang on tree.

Yield: 40 to 80 cookies, depending on size and thickness
Will keep: several months at room temperature

ROYAL ICING FOR DECORATING AND PAINTING

Royal icing is extremely versatile. It dries to a hard, shiny consistency, making it an excellent medium for piping decorations on baked, cooled cookies. Diluted with a little water, it can be painted on with a paintbrush to provide a hard, shiny finish. You can adjust the consistency as often as you like—loosen the icing by adding a little more egg white or water, stiffen it by adding more confectioners' sugar. Adding a few drops of food coloring will provide you with even more artistic choices.

The icing can be applied with a pastry bag; a reclosable plastic freezer bag with a corner snipped off; an icing spatula, toothpicks, a sponge, a brush, or even your fingers. You are the artist, so choose your own tools.

1 pound confectioners' sugar
3 large egg whites

¼ teaspoon cream of tartar

Equipment: *electric mixer*

1. Into a large bowl, press the confectioners' sugar through a large strainer to remove lumps.
2. In a medium-size bowl, beat the egg whites at medium speed just until they are frothy. Add sugar and cream of tartar, beat at low speed until sugar

and egg whites are mixed. Increase speed to high and beat until icing holds its shape (soft-peak stage). Icing should be of a consistency thick enough to hold its shape as it is being pressed through a tube, but not so thick as to make it difficult to pass through a tube. If it is too soft, it will run; if it is too thick, it will not adhere to cookies.

The consistency of the icing is easily adjusted. If it is too soft, add a little bit more confectioners' sugar to get desired consistency. If it is too thick, add water a few drops at a time.

3. Keep icing tightly covered with plastic wrap. It will keep for 3 days at room temperature. If it loses some of its body, beat it with a wire whisk or an electric mixer to restore desired consistency.

For piping: Scoop icing into a pastry bag fitted with a tube with a small opening, or scoop into a gallon-size plastic reclosable freezer bag. Squeeze icing into one corner and cut off a tiny snippet of the corner to make a hole through which to squeeze the icing.

For painting: Add water a few drops at a time, until you achieve desired consistency.

Our snow was not only shaken in whitewash buckets down the sky, I think it came shawling out of the ground and swam and drifted out of the arms and hands and bodies of the trees; snow grew overnight on the roofs of the houses like a pure and grandfather moss, minutely ivied the walls, and settled on the postman, opening the gate, like a dumb, numb thunderstorm of white, torn Christmas cards.

—Dylan Thomas

◆ JAN HAGEL COOKIES ◆

This is an almond-flavored, cinnamon-scented Christmas cookie from Holland. It is easy to make, keeps well, ships well, and is perfectly delicious. What else could anyone ask of a *koejke*, the Dutch word for *cookie*.

1½ cups all-purpose flour
½ cup sugar
½ cup sliced almonds
1 teaspoon ground cinnamon
1½ sticks sweet butter, refrigerator cold
1 teaspoon vanilla extract

Vanilla sugar for topping (page 122)

Equipment: *food processor; cookie sheets, lined with parchment paper or lightly greased; wire cooling racks*

1. In a food processor with a metal blade, combine flour, sugar, almonds, and cinnamon. Turn processor on, and drop in butter in small pieces. Add vanilla extract and process just until mixture resembles coarse meal.

2. Remove from processor onto a sheet of plastic wrap. Press dough firmly into a ball.

3. Divide dough in half and shape each portion into a log about 2 inches in diameter. Wrap each log well in plastic wrap and refrigerate for 2 hours or overnight.

4. Preheat oven to 375°F.

5. Cut cookie logs into ¼-inch slices and arrange 1 inch apart on prepared cookie sheets. Sprinkle cookies with vanilla sugar.

6. Bake 8 to 10 minutes, until cookies are lightly browned. Remove from oven and transfer cookies to wire racks to cool. Store completely cooled cookies in an airtight container.

Yield: about 3 dozen cookies
Will keep: several weeks at room temperature

Of course there were sweets. It was the marshmallows that squelched. Hardboileds, toffee, fudge and allsorts, crunches, cracknels, humbugs, glaciers, and marzipan and butterwelsh for the Welsh.

—Dylan Thomas

· PFEFFERNÜSSE ·

Pfeffernüsse, or *pepper nuts*, are traditional Central European Christmas cookies. They do contain a small amount of pepper, but in medieval recipes the word *pepper* was used to mean *spice*, and spices are what give these cookies their wonderful flavor. They should be baked several weeks to one month before Christmas. When they are first baked, Pfeffernüsse are as hard as the rocks they resemble, but as they mellow and ripen they become softer. A slice of apple is traditionally stored with the cookies to help them soften.

2 cups all-purpose flour
¼ teaspoon baking powder
1 teaspoon ground cinnamon
¼ teaspoon freshly ground pepper
¼ teaspoon ground cardamom
¼ teaspoon ground cloves
¼ teaspoon ground ginger
2 large eggs
1 cup sugar
½ cup finely chopped candied
  lemon peel (page 112)
or

Grated rind of 1 lemon
¼ cup finely ground almonds
⅓ cup rum or brandy
1 cup confectioners' sugar
1 apple slice

Equipment: *electric mixer; 1-inch-round cookie cutter; cookie sheets, lined with parchment paper or lightly greased and floured; wire cooling racks*

1. In a medium bowl, stir flour, baking powder, cinnamon, pepper, cardamom, cloves, and ginger with a wire whisk, to blend. Set aside.

2. In a large bowl, beat the eggs with an electric mixer on high speed until light and fluffy. Beat in sugar at high speed until mixture is thick and pale in color. On low speed, mix in candied lemon peel (or grated rind) and almonds. On very low speed, gradually beat in the flour mixture until just blended.

3. Scrape out dough onto a lightly floured surface. Dust your hands with flour and pat the dough out to a thickness of ¼ inch. Cut out cookies with a 1-inch-round cookie cutter and place them 1 inch apart on prepared cookie sheets. (Alternately, shape the dough into 1-inch balls, arrange on prepared cookie sheets, and press down balls with the bottom of a water glass dipped in sugar.) Let cookies rest, uncovered, in a cool dry place for 8 to 12 hours.

4. Preheat oven to 325°F.

5. Use an eye dropper or your fingertip to place 1 drop of rum or brandy in the center of each cookie. Bake for 15 to 20 minutes, until cookies are puffed and dry inside. Test by breaking one open to see if it is dry in the center.

6. Remove from oven and transfer cookies to wire racks to cool. While cookies are still warm, roll them in confectioners' sugar. Store completely cooled cookies in an airtight container with a slice of apple. Let ripen at least 2 weeks before eating.

Yield: 4 to 5 dozen cookies
Will keep: many months at room temperature

· FANCY LEMON BUTTER COOKIES ·

This is a very elegant, lovely cookie, vibrant with the taste of lemon, and so cheerfully reminiscent of sunny climes. It is an excellent cookie for mailing.

¾ cup sugar
2 sticks sweet butter
1 large egg
1 teaspoon vanilla extract
2 tablespoons lemon zest
2⅓ cups all-purpose flour

Toppings:
Lemon glaze (recipe follows)
Candied lemon zest (recipe follows)

Equipment: *food processor or electric mixer; cookie sheets, lined with parchment paper or ungreased cookie sheets; wire cooling racks*

1. In a food processor with a metal blade, process the sugar for several minutes until the texture of the sugar becomes very fine. With the processor on, add the butter in small pieces and process until smooth and creamy. Add the egg, vanilla extract, and lemon zest and pulse to incorporate. Scrape down sides of bowl, add flour, and process until just blended.

2. Scrape the dough onto a sheet of plastic wrap and divide in half. Roll each section of dough into a log about 1½ inches in diameter; wrap well in more plastic wrap. Chill in refrigerator for 2 hours or overnight.

3. Preheat oven to 350°F.

4. Slice dough into rounds ¼ inch thick. Place on prepared cookie sheets, leaving at least ½ inch space between rounds. Bake 8 to 10 minutes, until cookies begin to turn a light gold. Remove from oven and transfer cookies to

wire racks to cool. When cookies are completely cool, spread with lemon glaze and sprinkle with candied lemon zest. Let dry completely and store in an airtight container.

Yield: about 3 dozen cookies
Will keep: several weeks at room temperature

Using an electric mixer: Remove butter from refrigerator 30 minutes before using to soften. In a large bowl, cream butter with an electric mixer at medium speed. Increase speed and gradually beat in sugar. Continue beating until mixture is light and fluffy. Beat in egg, vanilla extract, and lemon zest. Scrape down sides of bowl. Reduce speed to low and beat in flour until just blended.

LEMON GLAZE

¼ cup fresh lemon juice
½ teaspoon grated lemon rind

½ teaspoon pure lemon extract
(optional)
1¼ cups confectioners' sugar

Place all ingredients in a bowl and stir until well blended and smooth.

CANDIED LEMON ZEST

Zest is the outer, colored layer of citrus fruit peels. Zest never includes the white part of the peel, called the "pith," which has a very bitter taste. Of all the citrus fruits, the zest of lemons seems to me to have the most vibrant taste. This same procedure will work with the zest of grapefruit, oranges, limes, and even tangerines. You might wish to consider buying organic fruit that has not been sprayed with insecticides or other poisons.

Candied lemon zest is called for in the recipe for Fancy Lemon Butter Cookies, but it is also wonderful on other glazed cookies, cheesecakes, or on your favorite butter cream cake.

3 bright, unblemished lemons,
preferably organic
½ cup sugar
¼ cup water

Equipment: *a vegetable peeler*

1. With a vegetable peeler, peel the zest from the lemons in the longest and widest pieces possible. Stack several pieces of zest one on top of the other and slice into fine julienne. The lengths of the pieces can vary.
2. Combine sugar and water in a small saucepan and bring to a boil, stirring occasionally. Continue boiling for 30 seconds or so until sugar is dissolved and syrup is clear. Add the zest; stir, and simmer for 2 to 3 minutes. Remove from heat and let zest cool in the syrup.
3. When cool, transfer to a small jar with a tight fitting lid and store in refrigerator. Remove from syrup as needed and drain on paper towel before using.

Yield: approximately ¼ cup
Will keep: 3 to 4 months in the refrigerator

Note: For a much plainer cookie, omit lemon glaze and candied lemon zest.
Sprinkle cookies with cinnamon sugar before baking.

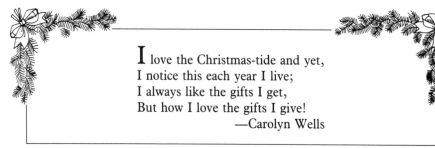

I love the Christmas-tide and yet,
I notice this each year I live;
I always like the gifts I get,
But how I love the gifts I give!
—Carolyn Wells

• ROSEMARY SHORTBREAD COOKIES •

If you don't have a pot of fresh rosemary sitting on your windowsill during the winter, go out right now and get one. Water it frequently and pinch back the leaves regularly to encourage it to flower. A flowering rosemary plant brings good luck to the entire household. Use the fresh rosemary to make these unusual and delicious cookies. And remember, for "rosemary" means *remembrance*, that a potted rosemary plant and a tin of these cookies makes a Christmas gift extraordinaire for a lucky person.

⅔ *cup granulated sugar*
2½ *sticks sweet butter*
2 *tablespoons finely minced fresh*
  rosemary needles
2½ *cups all-purpose flour*
2 *tablespoons granulated sugar, for*
  sprinkling

Equipment: *food processor; plain round or fluted-edge 2-inch cookie cutter; cookie sheets, lined with parchment paper or ungreased cookie sheets; wire cooling racks*

1. Preheat oven to 300°F.
2. In a food processor with a metal blade, process the sugar for several minutes until the texture of the sugar becomes very fine. With the processor on, add the butter in small pieces and process until smooth and creamy. Scrape down sides of bowl; add rosemary and flour and process just until mixture turns to crumbly bits.
3. Scrape out of food-processor bowl onto a lightly floured surface. Mash together into a ball. Knead until mixture just holds together.

4. Divide the dough into 2 equal parts. Pat each piece of dough into a flat disk; wrap well and refrigerate until cold, approximately 1 to 2 hours.

5. Roll the dough out on a well-floured pastry cloth or other floured surface to a ½-inch thickness. Cut out cookies using plain round or fluted 2-inch cookie cutter and place on cookie sheets. Sprinkle the tops of the cookies with granulated sugar.

6. Bake for 40 to 50 minutes, until cookies are pale gold in color. They should not brown. Remove from oven and transfer cookies to wire racks to cool. Store completely cooled cookies in an airtight container.

Yield: about 4 dozen cookies
Will keep: 1 month at room temperature

Heap on more wood!—the wind is chill;
But let it whistle as it will,
We'll keep our Christmas merry still.
—Sir Walter Scott

• ALMOND CRESCENTS •

There are many versions of this melt-in-your-mouth heavenly cookie. Greece, Austria, and Scandinavia all make a similar cookie to celebrate the winter holidays. My favorite recipe comes from Mrs. Bobs Strachan, a champion cookie baker in Ely, Minnesota.

2½ cups all-purpose flour
¼ teaspoon salt
¾ cup (¼ pound) blanched, sliced
*   almonds*
½ cup plus 1 tablespoon sugar
2 sticks plus 2 tablespoons sweet
*   butter, softened*
1 teaspoon vanilla extract

Topping:
1 cup superfine sugar

Equipment: *food processor; electric mixer; cookie sheets lined with parchment paper* or *foil; wire cooling racks*

1. In a small bowl, whisk together the flour and salt.

2. Place almonds and sugar in food processor. Using metal blade, process until almonds are very finely ground.

3. In a large bowl, cream butter with an electric mixer at medium speed. Increase speed and gradually beat in sugar-almond mixture and vanilla extract. Continue beating until mixture is light and fluffy. On low speed, beat in flour mixture until just incorporated.

4. Scrape the dough onto a sheet of plastic wrap. Flatten into a rough disk. Wrap tightly, and refrigerate for 2 hours or overnight.

5. Preheat oven to 350°F.

6. Divide dough into four parts. Refrigerate remaining dough while you work with each part.

7. Place the dough on a lightly floured surface and knead until dough is easy to work. Pinch off dough to roll into 1-inch balls. Roll each ball on floured surface to make a cylinder, and shape into a crescent.

8. Place crescents 1 inch apart on cookie sheet. Bake for 15 to 20 minutes, until cookies are set but not browned. Remove from oven; pull parchment paper or foil off hot cookie sheet onto wire racks, and allow cookies to rest for 10 to 12 minutes. Dunk warm cookies in superfine sugar and finish cooling on wire racks. Store in layers between sheets of wax paper in an airtight container.

Yield: about 5 dozen cookies
Will keep: 1 month at room temperature

• CHOCOLATE BROWNIE COOKIES •

These cookies are so delicious and disappear so quickly that no matter how many you bake, chances are you will not be able to keep up with the demand. If you plan to give them as gifts, make enough to survive frequent raids from resident cookie lovers. The basic recipe for this cookie comes from my friend Winifred Rosen. It is very much a chocolate lover's cookie, and very good for mailing.

1½ cups flour
1½ teaspoons baking powder
¼ teaspoon salt
3 ounces unsweetened chocolate,
*   chopped into small pieces*
6 tablespoons sweet butter
1 cup sugar
2 large eggs
1½ teaspoons vanilla extract

½ cup semisweet mini chocolate chips
½ cup chopped pecans
Confectioners' sugar

Equipment: *electric mixer; cookie sheets, lined with parchment paper or lightly greased; wire racks for cooling*

1. In a small bowl, whisk together the flour, baking powder, and salt. Set aside.

2. Melt chocolate in top of double boiler set over (but not touching) barely simmering water. When almost melted, remove from heat and stir until completely melted. Set aside.

3. In a large bowl, cream the butter with an electric mixer at medium speed. Raise speed to high, and gradually beat in the sugar. Continue beating

until mixture is light and fluffy. Beat in eggs, one at a time, until completely incorporated; beat in vanilla extract. Scrape down sides of bowl when necessary. Reduce beater speed to low, add melted chocolate, and beat until incorporated. Gradually beat in the flour mixture. Fold in chocolate chips and pecans. Cover bowl and refrigerate for 2 hours or overnight.

4. Preheat oven to 350°F.

5. Place confectioners' sugar in a small bowl. Shape cookie dough into balls about 1½ inches in diameter and dredge each ball in confectioners' sugar. Place 2 inches apart on prepared cookie sheet.

6. Bake for 10 minutes. Cookies are done when the tops have a cracked surface but still feel slightly underdone. Cookies will firm as they cool, and centers should remain slightly soft. Do not overbake or the bottoms will burn, causing a bitter flavor. Let cookies cool on cookie sheets for a minute or two, then transfer to wire racks to finish cooling. Store completely cooled cookies in an airtight container.

Yield: 4 to 5 dozen cookies
Will keep: 2 weeks at room temperature

• SAVORY CHEESE COOKIES •

These are not really cookies at all, but crisp, spicy crackers that are delicious as hors d'oeuvres and a glass of wine. Also serve them with soup or salad, or with a cup of tea to those who always prefer something sharp and spicy to something sweet. These cookies keep well and ship well, and I've never known anyone who wasn't delighted to receive a tin of these for Christmas.

1 cup all-purpose flour
½ teaspoon salt
½ teaspoon cayenne pepper, or to taste
¼ teaspoon freshly ground black pepper
½ pound extra-sharp cheddar cheese, cut into small pieces

1 stick butter, refrigerator cold

Equipment: *food processor; cookie sheets, lined with parchment paper or ungreased; wire cooling racks*

1. In a medium bowl, stir flour, salt, cayenne pepper, and black pepper with a wire whisk, to blend. Set aside.

2. In a food processor, process the cheese to the texture of small crumbs. Add flour mixture and pulse to blend. With the motor on, add butter in small pieces and process until the mixture is just blended.

3. Scrape out dough onto a piece of plastic wrap. Press into a log 1½ to 2 inches in diameter. Wrap well and refrigerate for 2 hours or overnight.

4. Preheat oven to 350°F.

5. Remove dough from refrigerator and slice into thin rounds (⅛ to ¼ inch

thick). Arrange 1 inch apart on prepared cookie sheets. Bake 8 to 10 minutes, until cookies are very lightly browned.

6. Remove from oven and transfer cookies to wire racks to cool. Store completely cooled cookies in an airtight container.

Yield: 50 to 60 cookies
Will keep: 1 month at room temperature

> I have often thought, says Sir Roger, it happens very well that Christmas should fall out in the middle of winter.
>
> —Addison

• CHOCOLATE TEDDY BEARS •

Who can resist a chocolate teddy bear? I like my bears very simple: silver dragées for eyes, nose, and buttons down the front. Press these into the cut-out cookies before baking. You can get as creative as you like. Trim them with icing, or use cinnamon red-hots, gold dragées, and so on.

Everybody on your list will enjoy receiving these enchanting cookies. Hang them from your tree, mail them to faraway friends and family, or tie them to the name tags on wrapped Christmas presents.

2½ cups all-purpose flour
2 teaspoons baking powder
½ cup unsweetened Dutch process
 cocoa
1 teaspoon cinnamon
¼ teaspoon salt
1 stick sweet butter, softened
1 cup sugar
2 large eggs
1 teaspoon pure vanilla extract

Decorating options:
Dragées, raisins, currants, cinnamon
 red-hots
Royal icing (page 85)
Ribbons

Equipment: *electric mixer; rolling pin; teddy bear cookie cutters* or *any other shapes you wish; cookie sheets, lined with parchment paper* or *lightly greased; wire cooling racks*

1. In a medium bowl, stir flour, baking powder, cocoa, cinnamon, and salt with a whisk, to blend. Set aside.

2. In a large bowl, cream butter with an electric mixer at medium speed. Increase speed and gradually beat in sugar. Continue beating until mixture

is light and fluffy. Beat in eggs, one at a time, and vanilla extract. On low speed, beat in flour mixture until just incorporated.

3. Divide dough in half and scoop out onto two sheets of plastic wrap. Using the plastic wrap, flatten the dough into 2 large disks, wrap tightly, and refrigerate for 2 hours or overnight.

4. Preheat oven to 375°F.

5. Remove dough from refrigerator. Dust rolling pin with flour and roll out dough on a lightly floured surface. Dough should be ¼ inch to ⅛ inch thick. The thinner the dough the crisper the cookies. Cut out bears with cookie cutters dipped in flour. If you wish to use the cookies as hanging ornaments, make a hole in each cookie with the blunt end of a bamboo skewer or plastic straw. Press dragées or other decorations into the dough for eyes, buttons, etc. Transfer to prepared cookie sheets with spatula.

6. Bake 8 to 10 minutes; cookies should feel springy when touched. Remove from oven and transfer cookies to wire racks to cool. If the holes in the cookies have closed up during baking, punch out again with blunt end of wooden skewer. Let cookies cool completely before decorating with icing. Let icing dry completely. Use ribbons or gold or silver elastics to suspend cookies from tree, or store in an airtight container.

Yield: 1 to 3 dozen cookies, depending on size of cutters
Will keep: 1 month at room temperature

Note: Use your bear cookie cutter to cut out bear-shaped cookies from the sugar cookie dough recipe on page 75. Press mini chocolate chips into the unbaked bears for eyes, nose, and buttons. The blond and brown bears make a wonderful combination in a gift tin or for Christmas tree ornaments.

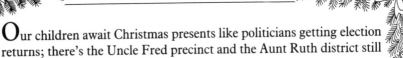

Our children await Christmas presents like politicians getting election returns; there's the Uncle Fred precinct and the Aunt Ruth district still to come in.

—Marcelene Cox

Confections and
Other Goodies

• CHOCOLATE TRUFFLES •

"Too good to be true" is what everyone says when they taste these very sophisticated chocolate confections. Also too good to be true is how quick and easy they are to make. The chocolate mixture requires about 4 hours in the refrigerator to cool and harden before you can roll out the truffles. Once you make the mixture, however, you can keep it on hand in the refrigerator for several weeks, ready to make instant truffles at a moment's notice.

1¼ cups heavy cream, scalded
12 ounces best-quality semisweet or
  bittersweet chocolate (preferably
  Lindt)
Topping: *1 cup hazelnuts*
¼ cup unsweetened cocoa

Equipment: *food processor; foil petit*
  four cups for serving (optional)

1. Preheat oven to 375°F.

2. In a small heavy saucepan, over medium heat, scald the cream. Remove from heat.

3. Break up the chocolate and process in a food processor with a metal blade until the particles are very small. With the food processor on, pour in hot cream and process until chocolate is melted and mixture is very smooth. Pour mixture into a container with a tight lid and refrigerate for 3 to 4 hours, until mixture is cold and solid.

4. Spread the hazelnuts in a single layer in a shallow baking pan and bake for 10 to 12 minutes, until nuts are almost too hot to touch. Remove from

oven. As soon as you can handle them, rub hazelnuts between the palms of your hands to remove as much of the black skin as possible. Some will remain, so don't worry about it. When hazelnuts are completely cool, grind them in a food processor or nut grinder to a fine powder. Set aside. (Turn off oven. You will not need it anymore.)

5. Spread a large sheet of wax paper on your work surface. Pour the ground hazelnuts in one pile, and the cocoa in another. Scoop a rounded teaspoonful of the chocolate mixture into your hand. Roll into a ball approximately 1 inch in diameter. Roll chocolate ball in hazelnuts, pressing nuts into the chocolate, then roll in cocoa. Place each ball inside a foil cup. Refrigerate until ready to serve.

Yield: 4 dozen truffles
Will keep: 1 week to 10 days in the refrigerator

• GENIE'S KENTUCKY BOURBON BALLS •

The strong, sweet flavors of Kentucky make these grown-up confections so delicious. The recipe come from Genie Chipps, whose family has made these delicacies at Christmastime for many generations. They are excellent for mailing and keeping on hand for holiday entertaining.

1 cup lightly toasted pecans
2½ cups crushed Vanilla Wafers
  (page 68)
1 cup confectioners' sugar
3 tablespoons light corn syrup

¼ cup Kentucky bourbon whiskey
Vanilla confectioners' sugar (page 123)

Equipment: *food processor*

1. In a food processor with a metal blade, process the pecans until coarsely ground. Add Vanilla Wafers and sugar and process to a fine texture. Add corn syrup and bourbon whiskey and pulse until just mixed. Remove to a mixing bowl. Let stand for a few minutes.

2. Form into balls 1 inch in diameter. Roll in confectioners' sugar and store in an airtight container, with wax paper between the layers. Let stand a few days before serving.

Yield: about 40 bourbon balls
Will keep: 1 week to 10 days at room temperature; many months in the refrigerator

Variation: For Rum Cocoa Balls, substitute dark rum for bourbon whiskey and add 2 tablespoons of unsweetened dutch process cocoa to the mixture.

• CANDIED CITRUS PEEL •

The candied peel of oranges, grapefruit, lemons, or limes makes delicious confections that are just the thing to nibble on after dinner with a cup of espresso. They are especially appreciated today when many people eschew rich desserts but miss the final burst of vivid sweet flavor to end a meal. Serve these for dessert in tiny foil cups at your dinner parties as part of a large cookie assortment. Little cups filled with candied cranberries (page 115) and candied ginger (page 117) are excellent companions. Packaged in a pretty jar these make wonderful gifts.

Follow these directions to candy the peel of any citrus fruit. It is important to prepare each type of citrus peel separately so as not to muddy the flavors. If at all possible, use organic fruit that has not been sprayed.

4 large oranges (navels are perfect)	*6 tablespoons light corn syrup*
or	*About 2 cups superfine sugar*
6 lemons or limes	*or*
or	*2 cups granulated sugar, processed in*
2 large grapefruit	*a food processor with a metal blade*
1½ cups sugar	*until the texture of the sugar*
1½ cups water	*becomes very fine*

1. Using a small sharp knife, cut away a small slice from the top and bottom of the fruit and score the skin into quarters. Peel away the skin, leaving the pith attached to it.

2. Place the peel in a saucepan and cover with water. Bring to a boil and

cook for 1 minute. Drain in a colander, rinsing with cold water. Repeat boiling, draining, rinsing twice more (3 times altogether). After the third rinsing, put peel back in saucepan, cover with water, and simmer for 20 minutes. Drain, rinse with cold water, and pat dry.

3. Cut the peel into ¼-inch slices.

4. Combine 1½ cups sugar, 1½ cups water, and 6 tablespoons light corn syrup in the saucepan and boil for 2 to 3 minutes. Add the peel slices, reduce heat to a simmer, and cook until almost all the syrup has boiled away. Do not let the sugar caramelize. Remove from heat.

5. Spread half the superfine sugar on a large platter or a baking sheet lined with wax paper. Use a fork to remove the peel from the saucepan and spread the peel on the sugar. Sprinkle remaining sugar over the citrus peels. Toss the peels around in the sugar as they cool.

6. When completely cool, put the strips in single layers on a cake rack to dry for 12 to 24 hours. Store in an airtight container or tightly sealed plastic bag.

Yield: about 1 pound
Will keep: 6 months to a year

Note: If you like your candied peel to be slightly soft and translucent, dry for a shorter period of time. The longer you dry the peel, the "harder" it will be candied and the longer it will keep.

Variation: For extravagant flavor and presentation, melt 4 ounces bittersweet or semisweet chocolate together with 1 tablespoon sweet butter in the top of a double boiler set over (but not touching) barely simmering water. When most of the chocolate has melted, remove from heat and stir until it has *all* melted. Dip one end of completely dry sugared peel into the chocolate and dry on wire rack. Continue until all the chocolate has been used up or you cannot do it any longer. This is painstaking work and should only be done for one who is much beloved or for yourself.

• CANDIED CRANBERRIES •

Candied cranberries are a wonderful sweetly tart substitute for glacé or maraschino cherries, but I like them best served as a confection with other desserts at the end of a fancy meal.

2 cups cranberries, picked over and
   rinsed
1½ cups sugar
1 cup superfine sugar
or
2 cups granulated sugar, processed
   in a food processor with a metal
   blade until the texture of the
   sugar becomes very fine

1. Place cranberries in a heat-proof bowl and set aside.
2. Combine 1½ cups sugar and 1 cup water in a small saucepan. Bring to a boil over high heat and stir until sugar dissolves.
3. Pour boiling syrup over the cranberries and mix well.
4. In a large pot or steamer, bring 2 inches of water to a simmer. Place the bowl containing cranberries on a steamer rack; cover, and steam for 40 minutes. Add more water to steamer if necessary.
5. Remove bowl of cranberries from the pot and let cool without stirring. Cover bowl with cheesecloth and let stand in a warm, dry room for 3 or 4 days. The syrup will become thick and slightly jelled.

6. Line 2 baking sheets with wax paper. Lift cranberries from syrup with a slotted spoon onto one of the baking sheets. (Reserve the syrup to use as topping for pancakes or to mix with soda water for a refreshing drink.) Place 1 cup superfine sugar in a bowl and roll each cranberry in the sugar. Place sugared berries on other baking sheet. Let berries dry for several hours, then dip in sugar again. Let dry until they are no longer sticky, preferably overnight. Store in a tightly closed jar.

Yield: about 1½ cups
Will keep: for many months

◆ CANDIED GINGER ◆

This confection is best made in the late summer or early fall months when it is possible to find very fresh, plump young ginger. If you have access to an oriental market, all the better to find the best selection. There, too, you will probably find Chinese yellow rock sugar, which will give the ginger a particularly lovely sheen and texture. Substitute ¼ pound Chinese yellow rock sugar for the honey and brown sugar called for in the recipe. Try to avoid ginger that is old, wrinkled, or in any way dried-up looking. The texture will be very tough and fibrous and the taste will be much too sharp.

Do serve candied ginger to your guests with after-dinner coffee. This is a centuries-old tradition and it is time to revive it. Guests who are avoiding rich desserts will be grateful for this delicious and satisfying nibble. And anyone who has overindulged in too much food will appreciate the way ginger helps settle the stomach.

Homemade candied ginger makes a wonderful gift.

1 pound fresh, smooth-skinned,
plump young ginger
1½ cups granulated sugar
1 cup honey
½ cup dark brown sugar

¼ teaspoon salt
Additional sugar for coating

Equipment: *wire cooling rack*

1. Break the ginger apart at the joints and cut away the peel with a small sharp knife. Slice the ginger, on the bias, into ¼-inch pieces.

2. Place ginger slices in a bowl, covered by 2 inches of cold water, and let stand overnight.

3. Drain the ginger slices and place in a large saucepan. Add enough water to cover by 1 inch. Bring to a boil over high heat, then reduce heat and simmer for 10 minutes. Drain the ginger, place back in saucepan, cover with cold water, and repeat the entire process 3 more times. After the fourth simmer, taste a piece of ginger to see if the sharpness is to your liking. If it is too sharp, repeat simmering and draining 2 or 3 more times.

4. Place granulated sugar, honey and brown sugar (or Chinese yellow rock sugar), and salt in the saucepan together with 2½ cups water. Bring to a boil over high heat, then reduce heat and simmer until the sugar is dissolved. Add the ginger and return to a boil, then reduce heat and simmer for 5 minutes. Remove saucepan from heat and let stand for several hours, or overnight, until the syrup and ginger are completely cool.

5. Place saucepan over low heat and simmer gently for 30 minutes to 1 hour, stirring frequently, until ginger becomes translucent and the syrup has almost completely boiled away. Watch carefully so the syrup and ginger do not burn. There should be almost no syrup left at the end.

6. Remove saucepan from heat and let cool for a few minutes. Remove ginger pieces with a fork to a wire rack and allow them to cool and dry completely. This will take several hours. Finally, toss the ginger pieces in granulated sugar to coat them lightly. Store in an airtight container.

Yield: about 1 pound
Will keep: indefinitely, if kept dry and airtight

• WALNUT BRITTLE •

The recipe for this nut candy comes from my friend Leah Fischer. It is one of the many sweets she serves at the end of a *seder*, when no dish may contain any flour. She uses margarine in her recipe, but I have substituted butter because I prefer its flavor. I like to pack Walnut Brittle with an assortment of other cookies and confections and give it as a Christmas or Hanukkah present.

3½ *cups broken-up walnut pieces*
1 *cup wildflower or other flavorful*
   honey
½ *cup light corn syrup*
4 *tablespoons sweet butter*
1 *tablespoon lemon juice*
¼ *teaspoon baking soda*

Equipment: 1 *ungreased baking*
   sheet; 2 baking sheets, greased with
   butter or *sprayed with nonstick*
   vegetable oil spray

1. Preheat oven to 350°F.

2. Spread walnut halves in a single layer on ungreased baking sheet and toast for 10 minutes, shaking the nuts around several times. Remove and let cool until you can handle the nuts. Rub nuts between your hands to remove any loose skin. Chop coarsely with a large sharp knife. (Turn off the oven. You will no longer need it.)

3. In a large, heavy saucepan, heat the honey, corn syrup, butter, and lemon juice over medium heat. Let boil for 10 minutes. Add walnuts and

baking soda and cook over low heat, stirring constantly, until the mixture darkens and thickens. Be careful not to let it burn.

4. Pour mixture out as thinly as possible onto 2 greased baking sheets. Spray a rubber spatula with nonstick vegetable oil spray or rub with butter, and spread the mixture to make it about ¼ inch thick. Allow brittle to cool and harden. When the brittle is hard, crack it into bite-size pieces. Store in an airtight container. Let ripen for 1 or 2 days before serving.

Yield: about 1½ pounds
Will keep: 1 month

Still xmas is a good time with all those presents and good food and i hope it will never die out or at any rate not until i am grown up and hav to pay for it all.

—Geoffrey Willans and Ronald Searle

• VANILLA BRANDY •

Look for pretty bottles and decanters at yard and rummage sales. In the fall, fill them with vanilla brandy. Tie a ribbon around the bottle and you'll have a perfect Christmas gift for every cook on your list. It can be used in any recipe that calls for pure vanilla extract.

*1 cup good brandy, cognac, or
    dark rum*
*1 vanilla bean, cut in half and
    split lengthwise*

*Small glass bottle or jar with tightly
    fitting lid*

Pour brandy into bottle or jar and add cut-up vanilla bean. The vanilla bean should be immersed. If pieces stick out, cut into smaller pieces. Cover with a tight lid and let stand for 1 month before using. Vanilla bean can be removed to make vanilla sugar. I like to leave it in.

Yield: ½ pint vanilla brandy
Will keep: indefinitely, at room temperature

· VANILLA SUGAR ·

This is not so much a recipe as a gentle reminder that this simple procedure, involving the work of 1 minute, will yield countless future rewards. The sugar does improve in flavor after several weeks, which is why it is so frustrating when you want some and you haven't remembered to prepare it. Put up in a pretty jar or canister, this sugar makes a welcome gift for any baker on your Christmas list. For a really elaborate gift, accompany the sugar with a small bottle of vanilla brandy (page 121).

Vanilla sugar can be used in any recipe that calls for vanilla flavoring, but you don't need to wait for baking day. Use it to sweeten coffee or tea for a wonderful flavor perk.

3 cups granulated sugar   *1 vanilla bean*

1. Pour the sugar into a glass or plastic container with a tightly fitting lid.
2. Cut the vanilla bean in half and split the two halves lengthwise. Scrape the seeds into the sugar, stirring all around with a fork. Bury the four pieces of vanilla pod in the sugar. Close tightly and store at room temperature in a dry place. The sugar will be quite flavorful in 24 hours, but will continue to grow in flavor over many weeks.

Yield: 3 cups vanilla sugar
Will keep: indefinitely, if kept tightly covered in a dry place

• VANILLA CONFECTIONERS' SUGAR •

Use vanilla confectioners' sugar in any recipe that calls for confectioners' sugar. When placed in a decorative jar or canister, this makes a perfect gift for any baker.

*1 pound (1 box) confectioners'
sugar, sifted through a strainer*

1 vanilla bean

1. Pour the sugar into a glass or plastic container with a tightly fitting lid.
2. Cut the vanilla bean in half and split the two halves lengthwise. Scrape the seeds into the sugar, stirring all around with a fork. Bury the four pieces of vanilla pod in the sugar. Close tightly and store at room temperature in a dry place. The sugar will be quite flavorful in 24 hours, but will continue to grow in flavor over many weeks.

Yield: 1 pound vanilla confectioners' sugar
Will keep: indefinitely, if kept tightly covered in a dry place

Mail Order Sources
for Equipment and
Supplies

Williams-Sonoma
Mail Order Department
P.O. Box 7456
San Francisco, California 94120–7456
(415) 421–4242

Maid of Scandinavia
3244 Raleigh Avenue
Minneapolis, Minnesota 55416
(800) 328–6722

The Bridge Company
214 East 52 Street
New York, New York 10022
(212) 688–4220

Chocolate Gallery
34 West 22 Street
New York, New York 10010
(212) 675–2253

The King Arthur Flour Baker's Catalogue
RR 2, Box 56
Norwich, Vermont 05055
(800) 827–6836

Index

Almonds
    cinnamon mandelbröt, 70–72
    crescents, 98–99
    orange-almond tuiles, 58–59
    rolled almond wafers, 32–33
Animal cookies, 12

Baking parchment, 17–18
Bourbon balls, Genie's Kentucky, 111
Brandy, vanilla, 121
Brittle, walnut, 119–120
Brownies
    best fudgy, 44–45
    chocolate brownie cookies, 100–101
Brown sugar, 20
Brushes, 19
Butter, 19
Butter cookies, fancy lemon, 92–93

Candied confections
    citrus peel, 112–114
    cranberries, 115–116
    ginger, 117–118
    lemon zest, 94–95
Caraway seed cookies, 66–67
Cheese, savory cheese cookies, 102–103

Choco-coco kisses, 48–49
Chocolate, 20
    best fudgy brownies, 44–45
    brownie cookies, 100–101
    dipping glaze, 49
    hazelnut macaroons, 50–51
    madeleines, 46–47
    teddy bears, 104–106
    truffles, 109–110
Chocolate chip cookies
    grown-up, 42–43
    oatmeal, raisin, cranberry, pecan,
        chocolate chip cookies, 62–63
Chocolate "Oh"s, Robyn's, 40–41
Christmas
    cookie traditions, 12
    surviving, by baking cookies, 3
Christmas trees, 12
Cinnamon mandelbröt, 70–72
Citrus peel, candied, 112–114
Cocoa, 20
Coffee meringue kisses, 52–53
Confectioners' sugar, 20
    vanilla, 123
Confections, 107–123
Cookie cutters, 16–17

Cookie press, 17
Cookies
  Christmas traditions, 12
  decorating, 75–79, 85
  equipment for making, 15–19
  freezing, 21–22
  getting organized for baking, 4–8
  ingredients, 19–21
  mail order sources for supplies, 125–127
  one-step, 23–72
  as ornaments, 11
  packaging, 9–10
  shipping, 5–6, 9
  storage, 4–5, 19, 21–22
  timetable for making, 7–8
  tips for making, 15
  two-step, 73–106
Cookie sheets, 17
Cookie tins, 9, 10, 19, 21–22
Cooling racks, 18
Cranberries
  candied, 115–116
  oatmeal, raisin, cranberry, pecan, chocolate chip cookies, 62–63
Crescents, almond, 98–99

Decorating cookies, 75–79, 85
Double boilers, 16

Eggs, 20
Egg yolk paint, 77–78

Electric mixers, 15
Equipment, 15–19
  mail order sources, 125–127

Flavorings, 20
Flour, 19
Food processors, 16
Freezing cookies, 21–22
Fudgy brownies, best, 44–45

Gift ideas, 10
Ginger, candied, 117–118
Gingerbread, 83–86
Ginger snaps, 38–39
Glaze
  chocolate dipping, 49
  lemon, 93
  milk, 78
Gold paint, 78, 82
Granulated sugar, 20

Hazelnuts, chocolate macaroons, 50–51
Hearts, raspberry linzer, 54–55

Icing, royal, 85–86
Ingredients, 19–21

Jam-filled thimble cookies, 56–57
Jan Hagel cookies, 88–89

Kentucky bourbon balls, Genie's, 111
Kisses
    choco-coco, 48–49
    coffee meringue, 52–53
    walnut, 64–65

Lace cookies, oatmeal, 34–35
Lemon
    candied lemon zest, 94–95
    fancy lemon butter cookies, 92–93
    glaze, 93
Linzers, raspberry hearts, 54–55
Liquid gold paint, 78, 82

Macaroons, chocolate hazelnut, 50–51
Madeleines, chocolate, 46–47
Mailing cookies, tips for, 9
Mail order sources of supplies, 125–127
Mandelbröt, cinnamon, 70–72
Maple walnut cookies, 36–37
Measuring cups, 16
Measuring spoons, 16
Meringue, coffee kisses, 52–53
Mexican Christmas Cookies, Ann
    Mann's, 30–31
Milk glaze, 78
Mixing bowls, 16

Nonstick vegetable cooking spray, 21
Nuts, 20
    almonds, 32–33, 58–59, 70–72,
        98–99
    hazelnuts, 50–51
    pecans, 62–63
    walnuts, 119–120

Oatmeal, 21
    Christmas cookies, 60–61
    lace cookies, 34–35
Oatmeal, raisin, cranberry, pecan,
    chocolate chip cookies, 62–63
"Oh"s, Robyn's chocolate, 40–41
Orange-almond tuiles, 58–59
Ornaments, cookies as, 11
Oven thermometers, 18

Packaging tips
    for hand delivery, 10
    for mail delivery, 9
Paint
    designs for, 79
    egg yolk, 77–78
    liquid gold, 78, 82
    royal icing, 85–86
Pastry bags, 17
Pastry cloth, 16
Pecans
    oatmeal, raisin, cranberry, pecan,
        chocolate chip cookies, 62–63
Peels, candied citrus, 112–114
Pfeffernüsse, 90–91
Plastic wrap, 19

Raisins
    oatmeal, raisin, cranberry, pecan,
       chocolate chip cookies, 62–63
Raspberry linzer hearts, 54–55
Rolled almond wafers, 32–33
Rolling pins, 16
Rosemary shortbread cookies, 96–97
Royal icing, 85–86
Rubber spatulas, 16

Saucepans, 16
Savory cheese cookies, 102–103
Shipping cookies
    packing tips, 9
    sturdy varieties, 5–6
Shortbread
    Christmas, 25–27
    rosemary cookies, 96–97
Sources for supplies, mail order, 125–
    127
Spatulas, 16, 18
Spoons, 16
Spray, nonstick, 21
Springerle cookies, 12, 80–82
Spritz cookies, fancy, 28–29
Storage of cookies, 19, 21–22
    cookies that store well, 4–5
Strainers, 18
Sugar, 20
    vanilla, 122
    vanilla confectioners', 123
Sugar cookies, old-fashioned, 75–79

Teddy bears, 104–106
Thimble cookies, jam-filled, 56–57
Timers, 18
Timetable for cooking making, 7–8
Traditions, based on Christmas cookies,
    12
Truffles, chocolate, 109–110

Vanilla
    brandy, 121
    confectioners' sugar, 123
    sugar, 122
    wafers, 68–69
Vanilla extract, 20

Wafers
    rolled almond, 32–33
    vanilla, 68–69
Walnuts
    brittle, 119–120
    kisses, 64–65
    maple walnut cookies, 36–37
Wax paper, 19
Whisks, 16
Winter festivals, 12
Wire cooling racks, 18
Wooden spoons, 16

Zest, candied lemon, 94–95